C000148329

SELECTED POEMS

BY THE SAME AUTHOR

POETRY

The Collector and Other Poems
The Nature of Cold Weather and Other Poems
At the White Monument and Other Poems
The Force and Other Poems
Work in Progress
Dr Faust's Sea-Spiral Spirit and Other Poems
Three Pieces for Voices
The Hermaphrodite Album (with Penelope Shuttle)
Sons of My Skin: Selected Poems 1954–74
From Every Chink of the Ark
The Weddings at Nether Powers
The Apple-Broadcast and Other New Poems
The Working of Water
The Man Named East and Other New Poems
The Mudlark Poems & Grand Buveur
The Moon Disposes: Poems 1954–1987
In the Hall of the Saurians
The First Earthquake
Dressed as for a Tarot Pack
Under the Reservoir
The Laborators
My Father's Trapdoors
Abyssophone
Assembling a Ghost
Orchard End

FICTION

In the Country of the Skin
The Terrors of Dr Treviles (with Penelope Shuttle)
The Glass Cottage
The God of Glass
The Sleep of the Great Hypnotist
The Beekeepers
The Facilitators, or, Madam Hole-in-the-Day
The One Who Set Out to Study Fear
The Cyclopean Mistress
What the Black Mirror Saw

PLAYBOOKS

Miss Carstairs Dressed for Blooding and Other Plays
In the Country of the Skin

PSYCHOLOGY AND SPIRITUALITY

The Wise Wound (with Penelope Shuttle)
The Black Goddess and the Sixth Sense
Alchemy for Women (with Penelope Shuttle)

SELECTED POEMS

Peter Redgrove

CAPE POETRY

Grateful acknowledgements are due to Robin Robertson,
who selected the poems.

Published by Jonathan Cape 1999

2 4 6 8 10 9 7 5 3 1

First published in Great Britain in 1999 by Jonathan Cape
Random House, 20 Vauxhall Bridge Road, London SW1V 2SA

Random House Australia (Pty) Limited
20 Alfred Street, Milsons Point, Sydney,
New South Wales 2061, Australia

Random House New Zealand Limited
18 Poland Road, Glenfield,
Auckland 10, New Zealand

Random House South Africa (Pty) Limited
Endulini, 5A Jubilee Road, Parktown 2193, South Africa

Random House UK Limited Reg. No. 954009

A CIP catalogue record for this book is available from the British Library

ISBN 0-224-06015-5 (paperback)
ISBN 0-224-06014-7 (hardback)

Typeset by Palimpsest Book Production Limited
Polmont, Stirlingshire

Printed and bound in Great Britain by
Biddles Ltd, www.biddles.co.uk

CONTENTS

from *In the Hall of the Saurians* (1987)

from *The First Earthquake* (1989)

from *Under the Reservoir* (1992)

from *My Father's Trapdoors* (1994)

from *Assembling a Ghost* (1996)

AGAINST DEATH

We are glad to have birds in our roof
Sealed off from rooms by white ceiling,
And glad to glimpse them homing straight
Blinking across the upstairs windows,
And to listen to them scratching on the laths
As we bed and whisper staring at the ceiling.
We're glad to be hospitable to birds.
In our rooms, in general only humans come,
We keep no cats and dislike wet-mouthed dogs,
And wind comes up the floorboards in a gale,
So then we keep to bed: no more productive place
To spend a blustery winter evening and keep warm.
Occasionally a spider capsizes in the bath,
Blot streaming with legs among the soap,
Cool and scab-bodied, soot-and-suet,
So we have to suffocate it down the pipe
For none of us'd have dealings with it,
Like kissing a corpse's lips, even
Through the fingers, so I flood it out.
In our high-headed rooms we're going to breed
Many human beings for their home
To fill the house with children and with life,
Running in service of the shrill white bodies,
With human life but for sparrows in the roof,
Wiping noses and cleaning up behind,
Slapping and sympathising, and catching glimpses
Of each other and ourselves as we were then,
And let out in the world a homing of adults.

And if there ever should be a corpse in the house
Hard on its bedsprings in a room upstairs,
Smelling of brass-polish, with sucked-in cheeks,
Staring through eyelids at a scratching ceiling,

I

Some firm'd hurry it outdoors and burn it quick –
We'd expect no more to happen to ourselves
Our children gradually foregoing grief of us
As the hot bodies of the sparrows increase each summer.

OLD HOUSE

I lay in an agony of imagination as the wind
Limped up the stairs and puffed on the landings,
Snuffled through floorboards from the foundations,
Tottered, withdrew into flaws, and shook the house.
Peppery dust swarmed through all cracks,
The boiling air blew a dry spume from other mouths,
From other hides and function:
Scale of dead people fountained to the ceiling –
What sort of a house is this to bring children to,

Burn it down, build with new-fired brick;
How many times has this place been wound up
Around the offensive memories of a dead person,
Or a palette of sick colours dry on the body,
Or bare arms through a dank trapdoor to shut off water,
Or windows filmed over the white faces of children:
'This is no place to bring children to'

I cried in a nightmare of more
Creatures shelled in bone-white,
Or dead eyes fronting soft ermine faces,
Or mantled in carnation, dying kings of creation,
Or crimson mouth-skirts flashing as they pass:
What a world to bring new lives into,

Flat on my back in a warm bed as the house around me
Lived in the wind more than the people that built it;
It was bought with all our earned money,
With all the dust I was nearly flying from my body
That whipped in the wind in this normal November,
And outstretched beside her in my silly agony
She turned in her sleep and called for me,
Then taught me what children were to make a home for.

Where did the voice come from? I hunted through the rooms
For that small boy, that high, that head-voice,
The clatter as his heels caught on the door,
A shadow just caught moving through the door
Something like a school-satchel. My wife
Didn't seem afraid, even when it called for food
She smiled and turned her book and said:
'I couldn't go and love the empty air.'

We went to bed. Our dreams seemed full
Of boys in one or another guise, the paper-boy
Skidding along in grubby jeans, a music-lesson
She went out in the early afternoon to fetch a child from.
I pulled up from a pillow damp with heat
And saw her kissing hers, her legs were folded
Far away from mine. A pillow! It seemed
She couldn't love the empty air.

Perhaps, we thought, a child had come to grief
In some room in the old house we kept,
And listened if the noises came from some especial room,
And then we'd take the boards up and discover
A pile of dusty bones like charcoal twigs and give
The tiny-sounding ghost a proper resting-place
So that it need not wander in the empty air.

No blood-stained attic harboured the floating sounds,
We found they came in rooms that we'd warmed with our life.
We traced the voice and found where it mostly came
From just underneath both our skins, and not only
In the night-time either, but at the height of noon
And when we sat at meals alone. Plainly, this is how we found
That love pines loudly to go out to where
It need not spend itself on fancy and the empty air.

MEMORIAL

David Redgrove: 28 December 1937–24 December 1957

Two photographs stand on the dresser
Joined up the spine. Put away
They fold until they kiss each other,
But put out, they look across the room.
My brother and myself. He is flushed and pouting
With heart, and standing square,
I, already white-browed and balding,
Float there, it seems, and look away.
You could look at us and say I was the one of air,
And he the brother of earth
Who, in Christmas-time, fell to his death.

Fancy, yes; but if you'd seen him in his life
There'd be his bright blond hair, and that flush,
And the mouth always slightly open, and the strength
Of body: those muscles! swelled up with the hard
    hand-springs at night

Certainly, but strong. I, on the other hand
Was remote, cross, and disengaged, a proper
Bastard to my brother, who enjoyed things,
Until he was able to defend himself. It's June;
Everything's come out in flush and white,
In ruff and sun, and tall green shoots
Hard with their sap. He's ashes
Like this cigarette I smoke into grey dryness.
I notice outside my window a tree of blossom,
Cherries, I think, one branch bending heavy
Into the grey road to its no advantage.
The hard stone scrapes the petals off,
And the dust enters the flower into its peak.

It is so heavy with flowers it bruises itself:
It has tripped, you might say, and fallen,
Cannot get up, so heavy with dust.
The air plays with it, and plays small-chess with the dust.

LAZARUS AND THE SEA

The tide of my death came whispering like this
Soiling my body with its tireless voice.
I scented the antique moistures when they sharpened
The air of my room, made the rough wood of my bed (most dear),

Standing out like roots in my tall grave.
They slopped in my mouth and entered my plaited blood
Quietened my jolting breath with a soft argument
Of such measured insistence, untied the great knot of my heart.

They spread like whispered conversations
Through all the numbed rippling tissues radiated
Like a tree for thirty years from the still centre
Of my salt ovum. But this calm dissolution
Came after my agreement to the necessity of it;
Where before it was a storm over red fields
Pocked with the rain and the wheat furrowed
With wind, then it was the drifting of smoke
From a fire of the wood, damp with sweat,
Fallen in the storm.

I could say nothing of where I had been,
But I knew the soil in my limbs and the rain-water
In my mouth, knew the ground as a slow sea unstable
Like clouds and tolerating no organisation such as mine
In its throat of my grave. The knotted roots
Would have entered my nostrils and held me
By the armpits, woven a blanket for my cold body
Dead in the smell of wet earth, and raised me to the sky
For the sun in the slow dance of the seasons.
Many gods like me would be laid in the ground
Dissolve and be formed again in this pure night
Among the blessing of birds and the sifting water.

But where was the boatman and his gliding punt?
The judgment and the flames? These happenings
Were much spoken of in my childhood and the legends.
And what judgment tore me to life, uprooted me
Back to my old problems and to the family,
Charged me with unfitness for this holy simplicity?

WITHOUT EYES

Today, to begin with, she will do without eyes.

Staring at the speckled ruby eyelids make of the sunny window
Now she tries the world with her eyelids closed;
Pulls the length of her body out of the rasp of sheets
Into her self-made night-time; delicately shuffles her way along the
    hairy carpet
To the cool rim she traces round with a finger.
Heaves the heavy bulging of the water-jug, tilts
And lets it grow lighter,
The tinkling in the bowl wax to a deep water-sound.
Sluices her bunched face with close hands, finds natural grease,
With clinking nails scrabbles for the body of the sprawling soap,
Rubs up the fine jumping lather that grips like a mask, floods it off,
Solving the dingy tallow.
Bloods and plumps her cheeks in the springy towel, a rolling
    variable darkness
Dimpling the feminine fat-pockets under the deep coombs of bone
And the firm sheathed jellies above that make silent lightning in
    their bulbs.

Moves to her clothes – a carpet-edge snatches her toe
Plucking the tacks sharply like flower-stalks from the boards but
Leaves her smirking in darkness. Dresses:
Cupped hands grip. The bridge chafes quickly over the thighs
And closes on the saddled groin,
Her silk dress thunders over her head and on to the flounced
    opening
Into quiet
And her eyes clip open on the ardent oblivion of her resolution and
The streets and clouds from her high window, swimming and
    dazzled, rush in.

GHOSTS

The terrace is said to be haunted.
By whom or what nobody knows; someone
Put away under the vines behind dusty glass
And rusty hinges staining the white-framed door
Like a nosebleed, locked; or a death in the pond
In three feet of water, a courageous breath?
It's haunted anyway, so nobody mends it
And the paving lies loose for the ants to crawl through
Weaving and clutching like animated thorns.
We walk on to it,
Like the bold lovers we are, ten years of marriage,
Tempting the ghosts out with our high spirits,
Footsteps doubled by the silence . . .

. . . and start up like ghosts ourselves
Flawed lank and drawn in the greenhouse glass:
She turns from that, and I sit down,
She tosses the dust with the toe of a shoe,
Sits on the pond's parapet and takes a swift look
At her shaking face in the clogged water,
Weeds in her hair; rises quickly and looks at me.
I shrug, and turn my palms out, begin
To feel the damp in my bones as I lever up
And step toward her with my hints of wrinkles,
Crows-feet and shadows. We leave arm in arm
Not a word said. The terrace is haunted,
Like many places with rough mirrors now,
By estrangement, if the daylight's strong.

CORPOSANT

A ghost of a mouldy larder is one thing: whiskery bread,
Green threads, jet dots,
Milk scabbed, the bottles choked with wool,
Shrouded cheese, ebony eggs, soft tomatoes
Cascading through their splits,
Whitewashed all around, a chalky smell,
And these parts steam their breath. The other thing
Is that to it comes the woman walking backwards
With her empty lamp playing through the empty house,
Her light sliding through her steaming breath in prayer.

Why exorcise the harmless mouldy ghost
With embodied clergymen and scalding texts?
Because she rises shrieking from the bone-dry bath
With bubbling wrists, a lamp and steaming breath,
Stretching shadows in her rooms till daybreak
The rancid larder glimmering from her corpse
Tall and wreathed like moulds or mists,
Spoiling the market value of the house.

MORE LEAVES FROM
MY BESTIARY

I SPIDER

Now, the spires of a privet fork from the hedge
And stretch a web between them;
The spider-nub eases his grip a trifle, twists a thread safe,
And the afternoon is quiet again.

Damp clouds drift above him; a burst of rain
Runs him back along a vane
To a leaf-shed, while it beads his web
And raises weed-smells from below
Of vetch, fumitory, and small mallow.

Hanging there are a dozen or so
Brown shells which tremble.
The curtain is ripped from the sun, and grass again
Leaps into its fumble:

Ants totter with their medicine balls and cabers, stone walls
Pop with their crickets;
A bluefly, furry as a dog, squares up
To the web and takes it with a jump like a hoop

And spider springs round like a man darting
To the fringes of a dogfight;

Tugging like a frantic sailor, buzzing like a jerky sawyer,
Fly finishes in swaddling
Tight as a knot
From the spinnerets' glistening.

And though spider
Hangs a little lower than the sun
Over all their heads, all
Seem ignorant of that passing;
The afternoon, the ebullience increases
Among the low boughs of the weeds
And spider steady, like a lichened glove
Only a little lower than the sun; none
Takes account of that to and fro passing,
Or of the manner of that death in swaddling.

II BASILISK

Rising above the fringe of silvering leaves
A finger, tanned and scaly, gorgeous, decayed,
Points to the shivering clouds, then turns down
Most slowly, towards you. The light catches, cold and hard
Pulls round the polished bone of fingernail
Arrests attention, the prey falls dead.

Bone mirrors have the quickest way to die
The sunlight loses strength and sap drained
Out and lost, distils a beam of purest mortality
Set in the velvet sockets of a fabled bird.
A mandarin of birds, exalted, alone
Sweeping its cold avenue of dying trees
Its restlessness oppressed for new fuel, warm
And busy not to lift its eyes, unrealised sin
Committed out of favour, and it dies.

But when it dies the silks collapse and draw aside.
The idle naturalist to draw this legend to its wisest close,
Pries. The walking-stick at first disturbs a swarm
But no danger from the tawny ground, it lies
As still as where it dropped. Newspaper and a spade

A tin tray in the quietest room; probes,
Licks like an eagle with his sharpest knives.
Fat, flesh, yes, and normal bones
Sincerely documented, the head from behind now
The brain, enlarged, hard and crisp as ice
No poison, the smell of preservatives, the face
At last, nostrils and beak, a wrinkled neck,
The eyelids closed. He pulls these aside,
They rustle, a smell like pungent spice

He catches. How curious, the eyes as dead
And white as buttons, hard, adamantine, he tries
To scratch them with his knife, with no effect,
Revolves the problem in his clouding head.
Then the light catches, and he dies.

EXPECTANT FATHER

Final things walk home with me through Chiswick Park,
Too much death, disaster; this year
All the children play at cripples
And cough along with one foot in the gutter.
But now my staircase is a way to bed
And not the weary gulf she sprinted down for doorbells
So far gone on with the child a-thump inside;
A buffet through the air from the kitchen door that sticks
Awakes a thumb-size fly. Butting the rebutting window-pane
It shouts its buzz, so I fling the glass up, let it fly
Remembering as it skims to trees, too late to swat,
That flies are polio-whiskered to the brows
With breeding-muck, and home
On one per cent of everybody's children.

So it is the week when Matron curfews, with her cuffs,
And I draw back. My wife, round as a bell in bed, is white and happy.

Left to myself I undress for the night
By the fine bright wires of lamps; hot tips
To burrowing cables, the bloodscheme of the house,
Where flame sleeps. That,
With a shallow on the mattress from last night,
Is enough to set me thinking on fired bones
And body-prints in the charcoal of a house, how
Darkness stands for death, and how afraid of sleep I am;
And fearing thus, thus I fall fast asleep.

But at six o'clock, the phone rings in – success!
The Sister tells me our son came up with the sun:
It's a joke she's pleased to make, and so am I.
I see out of the window it's about a quarter high,
And promises another glorious day.

15

TWO POEMS

I SPRING

To pass by a pondbrink
Trodden by horses
Where among the green horsetails
Even the hoofprints
Shiver with tadpoles
Comma'd with offspring
And moist buds flick awake
On breeze-floundering sallows.

II EPHEMERID

The fly is yellowed by the sun,
Her plating heaves, her wings hum,
Her eyes are cobbled like a road,
Her job is done, her eggs are stowed
No matter in what. The sun
Yellows the hemlock she sits upon;
Her death is near, her job is done,
Paddling in pollen and the sun,
She swings upon the white-flowered weed,
As a last duty, yellow with seed,
She falters round the flower-rim,
Falters around the flower-rim.

THE HOUSE IN THE ACORN

Ah, I thought just as he opened the door
That we all turned, for an instant, and looked away,
Checked ourselves suddenly, then he spoke:
'You're very good to come,' then,
Just for a moment his air thickened,
And he could not breathe, just for the moment.
'My son would have been glad that you came,'
He extended his thick hand, 'Here, all together –'
We are not ourselves or at our ease,
I thought, as we raised our glasses, sipped;
'Help yourselves, please. Please . . .'

'If anyone would care . . .' He stood by the table
Rapping his heavy nails in its polished glare,
'My son is upstairs, at the back of the house,
The nursery, if anyone . . .' I studied
Stocky hair-avenues along my hand-backs,
Wandered through grained plots dappled and sunlit;
'My son . . . sometimes I think they glimpse
Perhaps for a while through sealed lids a few faces
Bending in friendship before it all fades . . .' I nodded,
Slipped out, face averted,

And entered oak aisles; oaken treads
Mounted me up along oaken shafts, lifting me past
Tall silent room upon silent room:
Grained centuries of sunlight toppled to twilight
By chopping and fitting: time turned to timber
And the last oak enclosure with claws of bent oak
Where his white wisp cradled, instantaneous,
Hardly held by his home in its polished housetops.
A breath would have blown him; I held my breath
As I dipped to kiss . . .

Now the instant of this house rolls in my palm
And the company spins in its polished globe
And the drawing-room reels and the house recedes
(Pattering dome-grained out of the oak)
While, ah, as I open the door I hear their close laughter,
Cool earrings swing to the gliding whisper,
More apple-cup chugs from the stouted ewer.

THE FORCE

At Mrs Tyson's farmhouse, the electricity is pumped
Off her beck-borne wooden wheel outside.
Greased, steady, it spins within
A white torrent, that stretches up the rocks.
At night its force bounds down
And shakes the lighted rooms, shakes the light;
The mountain's force comes towering down to us.

High near its summit the brink is hitched
To an overflowing squally tarn.
It trembles with stored storms
That pulse across the rim to us, as light.

On a gusty day like this the force
Lashes its tail, the sky abounds
With wind-stuffed rinds of cloud that sprout
Clear force, throbbing in squalls off the sea
Where the sun stands poring down at itself
And makes the air grow tall in spurts
Whose crests turn over in the night-wind, foaming. We spin
Like a loose wheel, and throbbing shakes our light
Into winter, and torrents dangle. Sun
Pulls up the air in fountains, green shoots, forests
Flinching up at it in spray of branches,
Sends down clear water and the loosened torrent
Down into Mrs Tyson's farmhouse backyard,
That pumps white beams off its crest,
In a stiff breeze lashes its tail down the rocks.

SWEAT

I sit in the hot room and I sweat,
I see the cool pane bedew with me,
My skin breathes out and pearls the windowpane,
Likes it and clings to it. She comes in,
She loves me and she loves our children too,
And still the sweat is trickling down the pane,
The breath of life makes cooling streaks
And wobbles down the pane. We breathe and burn,
We burn, all together in a hot room,
Our sweat is smoking down the windowpane,
Marks time. I smoke, I stir, and there I write
PR, BR, a streaming heart.
The sun strikes at it down a wide hollow shaft;
Birds swing on the beams, boil off the grass.

THE CASE

for Roy Hart

'Man . . . is an experiment and a transition. He is nothing else than the
narrow and perilous bridge between nature and spirit. His innermost
destiny drives him on to the spirit and to God. His innermost longing
draws him back to nature, the mother. Between the two forces his
life hangs tremulous and irresolute.'

(Hermann Hesse, *Steppenwolf*)

I am a gardener,
A maker of trials, flowers, hypotheses.
I water the earth.
I raise perfumes there.
Mother told me to stand, and I did so,
Stepping towards the window in which she sat.
'Now, did you find him, your other half?
And mine,' she said, and I shook my head:
'No, my time is so short and I'll take no oath.'
'You've just taken one, by standing,
My dear one,' she said, and she told me how the stars
Had said as much, and I concurred and saw
How the crystalware of the polished table,
The cabinets of glass things walling the room,
The tall roses beyond the glass, the gloss of the table,
Had said as much in sunshine from my first tottering.
So she lifted my hand and kissed it and said I was to be celibate,
And this was great good fortune and I was a good child
For I had a quest and few had as much.
The roses nodded.

So I became a gardener,
A maker of prayers, flowers, hypotheses.
A gardener 'washed in my fertile sweat',
My hair of an opulent brown 'like the Lord's,
That makes you think of fertile fields.'
And among the flowers, in the walled garden, 'This is life!'
   she cried,

'What a shame, oh what a shame,' she said,
'What a shame we have to die,' she cried, all
The flowers pumping and pumping their natures into her,
Into her nostrils, winged wide, she leaning,
Leaning back, breathing deeply, blushing deeply,
Face shining and deep breath and tall brick
Holding the air still and the heat high in a tall room.

And I swam in the thunderstorm in the river of blood, oil
   and cider,
And I saw the blue of my recovery open around me in the water
Blood, cider, rainbow, and the apples still warm after sunset
Dashed in the cold downpour, and so this mother-world
Opened around me and I lay in the perfumes after rain out of
   the river
Tugging the wet grass, eyes squeezed, straining to the glory,
The burst of white glory like the whitest clouds rising to the sun

And it was like a door opening in the sky, it was like a door
   opening in the water,
It was like the high mansion of the sky, and water poured from the
   tall french windows.
It was like a sudden smell of fur among the flowers, it was like a
   face at dusk
It was like a rough trouser on a smooth leg. Oh, shame,
It was the mother-world wet with perfume. It was something
   about God.

And she stood there and I wanted to tell her something and she
    was gone
It was something about God. She stood smiling on the wet verge
And she waited for me to tell her but she was gone.
And three gusts of hot dry air came almost without sound
Through the bushes, and she went. Through the bushes
Of blown and bruised roses. And she went. And the bushes
    were blown
And the gusts were hot, dry air, nearly black with perfume,
Alive with perfume. Oh shame. It was like an announcement,
Like an invitation, an introduction, an invitation, a quick smile in
    the dusk.
It was like a door opening on a door of flowers that opened on
    flowers that were opening.
It was like the twist of a rosy fish among lily-pads that were
    twisting on their deep stems.
The rosy goldfish were there in the dusky pond, but she was gone.
It was something about God. My hand made a wet door in
    the water
And I thought of something I knew about God. My mother
Stared at me from the pool over my shoulder and when I turned
    she was gone.
Then the wind blew three hot dry gusts to me through the broken
    rose-bushes
And she came to me dusky with perfume and I walked toward her
And through her, groping for her hand. And it was something
    about God.
And I searched in my head for it with my eyes closed. But it
    was gone.

And I became a gardener, a hypothesiser, one who would consult
  his sensations,
For 'we live in sensations and where there are none there is no life,'
One with the birds that are blue-egged because they love the sky!
With the flocks of giraffes craning towards the heavens!
With the peacocks dressed in their love for the high sun
And in their spectra of the drifting rains, one
With the great oaks in my keeping that stretched up to touch God!
And one who could look up gladly and meet God's gaze,
His wide blue gaze, through my blood, as I think;
And God was silent and invisible and I loved him for it,
I loved him for his silent invisibility, for his virile restraint,
And I was one with my peacocks that sent out their wild cry
Sounding like shrill 'help!' and meaning no such thing,
While my flocks of deer wrote love in their free legs
Their high springy haunches and bounding turf. And they
  would pause
And look upwards, and breathe through wide nostrils, and all day
It was wide and firm and in God's gaze and open: tussock and turf,
  long lake,
Reed-sigh, silence and space, pathway and flower furnace
Banked up and breathing.

And the people. And the causeway into the walled garden.
And the people walking in so slowly, on their toes
Through the wide doorway, into the cube of still air,
Into the perspective of flowers, following each other in groups,
Gazing around, 'Oh, what shame, to die!' and the great doorway
And ourselves, smiling, and standing back, and they changed,
Concentrated, concentrating, at the edges of the body, the rims
Tighter, clearer, by the sensations of their bodies, solidified, bound,
Like the angels, the bodies' knowledge of the flowers inbound
Into its tightening and warming at the heart of flowers, the fire called
'Then-shall-ye-see-and-your-heart-shall-rejoice-
And-your-bones-shall-sprout-as-the-blade . . .'

And she was gone. And she lay down like the earth after rain.
It was love-talk in every grain. And something about God.

The brick walls creaked in the wind, grain to grain.
And judgment came as the father comes, and she is gone.
Clouds swoop under the turf into the pond, the peacock cries
'Help!' strutting in its aurora, love talks
Grain to grain, gossiping about judgment, his coming. Ranges
Tumble to boulders that rattle to shingles that ease to wide beaches
That flurry to dust that puffs to new dusts that dust
To dusting dust, all talking, all
Gossiping of glory, and there are people
In the gardens, in white shirts, drifting,
Gossiping of shame through the gardens, 'Oh glory!'

Through the gardens . . . Well, father, is that how you come?
Come then.
Whose breath is it that flares through the shrubberies?
Whose breath that returns? Look at the people
All ageing to judgment, all
Agreeing to judgment. Look at that woman
Still snuffing up the flowers. My mother!
Look at her. She bends backwards to the tall flowers, falls.
Her flower-laden breath returns to the skies.
I think this garden is a prayer,
Shall I burn it as an offering?
And I think these people are a prayer,
I think they are a message.
Shall I burn them for their syllable?
There is a fire crying 'shame!' here already!
It mixes dying with flowering.
I think we husk our uttering. I think
We tip it out. Our perfect syllable,
Tripped out over the death-bed, a one,
Round, perfectly-falling silence.

Look how they seek the glory over these flowers!
I wanted to say something about God,
My syllable about God. I think

We are a prayer. I think
He wants his breath back, unhusked
Of all the people, our dying silences,
Our great involuntary promise
Unhusked, flying out into the rain, over the battlefields,
Switching through shrubberies, into the sky . . .

You press, oh God!
You press on me as I press on an eyeball,
You press sunsets and autumns and dying flowers,
You press lank ageing people in gardens 'Oh shame
To die,' you feather roses and matchflames like wisps of
    your fingers,

Your great sun cuffs age at us. I will bring,
I will bring you in, father, through the bounds of my senses,
Face to face, father, through the sockets of my head,
Haul you in, father, through my eyes with my fingers,
Into my head through my eyes, father, my eyes, oh my eyes . . .

To live in the blind sockets, the glorious blunt passages,
Tended by gardeners, nostril, eye, mouth,
Bruised face in a white shirt ageing,
To be called 'Father' and to hear call high
'Oh shame, what a shame, to die' as they see the great flowers,
To hear the peacock 'help!' that means no such thing,
And to live unseeing, not watching, without judging, called
    'Father'.

MINERALS OF CORNWALL,
STONES OF CORNWALL

A case of samples

Splinters of information, stones of information,
Drab stones in a drab box, specimens of a distant place,
Granite, galena, talc, lava, kaolin, quartz,
Landscape in a box, under the dull sky of Leeds –
One morning was awake, in Cornwall, by the estuary,
In the tangy pearl-light, tangy tin-light,
And the stones were awake, these ounce-chips,
Had begun to think, in the place they came out of.

Tissues of the earth, in their proper place,
Quartz tinged with the rose, the deep quick,
Scrap of tissue of the slow heart of the earth,
Throbbing the light I look at it with,
Pumps slowly, most slowly, the deep organ of the earth;
And galena too, snow-silvery, its chipped sample
Shines like sun on peaks, it plays and thinks with the mineral light,
It sends back its good conclusions, it is exposed,
It sends back the light silked and silvered,
And talc, and kaolin, why they are purged, laundered,
As I see the white sand of some seamless beaches here
Is laundered and purged like the whole world's mud
Quite cleansed to its very crystal; talc a white matt,
Kaolin, the white wife of Cornwall
Glistening with inclusions, clearly its conclusions
Considered and laid down, the stone-look
Of its thoughts and opinions of flowers
And turf riding and seeding above it in the wind,
Thoughts gathered for millennia as they blossomed in millions
Above its then kaolin-station within the moor,
The place of foaming white streams and smoking blanched mountains.

Asbestos had found this bright morning
Its linear plan of fibres, its simple style,
Lay there, declaring, like the others;
Granite, the great rock, the rock of rocks,
At home now, flecked green, heavily contented in its box,
Riding with me high above its general body,
The great massif, while its fellows, the hills of it
Rise high around us; nor was lava silent
Now it remembered by glistening in this light
Boiling, and was swart with great content

Having seen God walking over the burning marl, having seen
A Someone thrusting his finger into the mountainside
To make it boil – here is the issue of this divine intrusion,
I am the issue of this divine intrusion,
My heart beats deep and fast, my teeth
Glisten over the swiftness of my breath,
My thoughts hurry like lightning, my voice
Is a squeak buried among the rending of mountains,
I am a mist passing through the crevices of these great seniors
Enclosed by me in a box, now free of the light, conversing
Of all the issue this homecoming has awakened in the stone mind
The mines like frozen bolts of black lightning deep in the land
Saying, and the edge of their imaginings cuts across my mind:
We are where we were taken from, and so we show ourselves
Ringing with changes and calls of fellowship
That call to us ton to ounce across Cornish valleys.

The valleys throng with the ghosts of stone so I may scarcely pass,
Their loving might crush, they cry out at their clumsiness,
Move away, death-dealing hardnesses, in love.
The house is full of sound of running water,
The night is a black honey, crystals wink at the brim,
A wind blows through the clock, the black mud outside
Lies curled up in haunches like a sleeping cat.

THE MOON DISPOSES

(Perranporth beach)

The mountainous sand-dunes with their gulls
Are all the same wind's moveables,
The wind's legs climb, recline,
Sit up gigantic, we wade
Such slithering pockets our legs are half the size,
There is an entrance pinched, a plain laid out,
An overshadowing of pleated forts.
We cannot see the sea, the sea-wind stings with sand,
We cannot see the moon that swims the wind,
The setting wave that started on the wind, pulls back.

Another slithering rim, we tumble whirling
A flying step to bed, better than harmless,
Here is someone's hoofprint on her hills
A broken ring with sheltering sides
She printed in the sand. A broken ring. We peer from play.

Hours late we walk among the strewn dead
Of this tide's sacrifice. There are strangled mussels:
The moon pulls back the lid, the wind unhinges them,
They choke on fans, they are bunched blue, black band.
The dead are beautiful, and give us life.
The setting wave recoils
In flocculence of blood-in-crystal,
It is medusa parched to hoofprints, broken bands,
Which are beautiful, and give us life.
The moon has stranded and the moon's air strangled
And the beauty of her dead dunes sent us up there
Which gave us life. Out at sea
Waves flee up the face of a far sea-rock, it is a pure white door
Flashing in the cliff-face opposite,
Great door, opening, closing, rumbling open, moonlike
Flying open on its close.

THE IDEA OF ENTROPY AT MAENPORTH BEACH

'C'est Elle! noire et pourtant lumineuse.'
to John Layard

A boggy wood as full of springs as trees.
Slowly she slipped into the muck.
It was a white dress, she said, and that was not right.
Leathery polished mud, that stank as it split.
It is a smooth white body, she said, and that is not right,
Not quite right; I'll have a smoother,
Slicker body, and my golden hair
Will sprinkle rich goodness everywhere.
So slowly she backed into the mud.

If it were a white dress, she said, with some little black,
Dressed with a little flaw, a smut, some swart
Twinge of ancestry, or if it were all black
Since I am white, but – it's my mistake.
So slowly she slunk, all pleated, into the muck.

The mud spatters with rich seed and ranging pollens.
Black darts up the pleats, black pleats
Lance along the white ones, and she stops
Swaying, cut in half. Is it right, she sobs
As the fat, juicy, incredibly tart muck rises
Round her throat and dims the diamond there?
It is right, so she stretches her white neck back
And takes a deep breath once and a one step back.
Some golden strands afloat pull after her.

The mud recoils, lies heavy, queasy, swart.
But then this soft blubber stirs, and quickly she comes up
Dressed like a mound of lickerish earth,
Swiftly ascending in a streaming pat
That grows tall, smooths brimming hips, and steps out
On flowing pillars, darkly draped.
And then the blackness breaks open with blue eyes
Of this black Venus rising helmeted in night
Who as she glides grins brilliantly, and drops
Swatches superb as molasses on her path.

Who is that negress running on the beach
Laughing excitedly with teeth as white
As the white waves kneeling, dazzled, to the sands?
Clapping excitedly the black rooks rise,
Running delightedly in slapping rags
She sprinkles substance, and the small life flies!

She laughs aloud, and bares her teeth again, and cries:
Now that I am all black, and running in my richness
And knowing it a little, I have learnt
It is quite wrong to be all white always;
And knowing it a little, I shall take great care
To keep a little black about me somewhere.
A snotty nostril, a mourning nail will do.
Mud is a good dress, but not the best.
Ah, watch, she runs into the sea. She walks
In streaky white on dazzling sands that stretch
Like the whole world's pursy mud quite purged.
The black rooks coo like doves, new suns beam
From every droplet of the shattering waves,
From every crystal of the shattered rock.
Drenched in the mud, pure white rejoiced,
From this collision were new colours born,
And in their slithering passage to the sea
The shrugged-up riches of deep darkness sang.

THE HALF-SCISSORS

Humming water holds the high stars.
Meteors fall through the great fat icicles.
Spiders at rest from skinny leg-work
Lean heads forward on shaggy head-laces
All glittering from an askew moon in the sky:
One hinge snapped; a white door dislocated.
The night leans forward on this thin window;
Next door, tattered glass,
Wind twittering on jagged edges.
Doors beat like wings wishing to rise.
I lean forward to this thin fire.
A woman leaves – even the flames grow cool –
She is a one hinge snapped, I am a half-scissors.

YOUNG WOMEN WITH THE
HAIR OF WITCHES AND
NO MODESTY

'I loved Ophelia!'

I have always loved water, and praised it.
I have often wished water would hold still.
Changes and glints bemuse a man terribly:
There is champagne and glimmer of mists;
Torrents, the distaffs of themselves, exalted, confused;
And snow splintering silently, skilfully, indifferently.
I have often wished water would hold still.
Now it does so, or ripples so, skilfully
In cross and doublecross, surcross and countercross.
A person lives in the darkness of it, watching gravely;

I used to see her straight and cool, considering the pond,
And as I approached she would turn gracefully
In her hair, its waves betraying her origin.
I told her that her thoughts issued in hair like consideration
    of water,
And if she laughed, that they would rain like spasms of weeping,

Or if she wept, then solemnly they held still,
And in the rain, the perfumes of it, and the blowing of it,
Confused, like hosts of people all shouting.
In such a world the bride walks through dressed as a waterfall,
And ripe grapes fall and splash smooth snow with jagged purple,
Young girls grow brown as acorns in their rainy climb towards
    oakhood,
And brown moths settle low down among ivories wet with love.
But she loosened her hair in a sudden tangle of contradictions,
In cross and doublecross, surcross and countercross,
And I was a shadow in the twilight of her late displeasure.
I asked water to stand still, now nothing else holds.

SIX ODES

I TABLE-LADY

I sent her into the wine-glass to listen.

I prodded her into the apple-burrow; I told her to take out her
pin-dagger as soon as she heard the maggot chewing.

I gave her a bath in a walnut-shell.

She made a salt-necklace, piercing the crystals together.

I was frightened when she fell into the mustard, but I rolled her
clean on a piece of bread.

I told her to sit in the cruet like an information kiosk and answer
some questions.

I compiled a savoury blanc-mange for her studded with angelica; it
was a gobbet of my fish-sauce.

But she ran from the reek of my steak, the evisceration of an
elephant; I gave her a cress-leaf fan.

She got drunk in a grape. I found her snoring like a scarlet fly on
her back in the skin like a flabby canoe.

It was after I had eaten the blood-orange that I missed her.

II WATER-LADY

He asked her to go into the wood and tell him what she saw there.

She walked between the trees and the first thing she liked was
the pond.

She knelt down and stripped off the thin film of reflections,
rolled it up and put it into her pocket to show she had
been there.

The water's new skin reflected with more brilliance and better colour.

So she knelt down and took this new skin and put it into her
pocket, throwing the other skin away.

But the colours of the newest skin were without equal so she took
this instead.

In due time she emptied the pond in this manner.

34

All that was left was a slippery hole, a sloppy quag with a few fish
    skipping.
She felt sorry for the fish so she went down into the quag and
    captured them in her skirt and climbed out.
Then she looked for where the torn scraps of reflection
    had settled among the undergrowth and she slid a fish into
    each one.
After she had done this she went back to him. 'What are those
    stains on your skirt?' were his first words . . .
But his suspicions were drowned in amazement as she unrolled the
    tapestry of reflections for him.

III HOWDAH–LADY

A little bloodstained clockwork in a puddle of blood.
She picked it up sighing, wiped it on her skirt.
Look, she said, it's all that's left of Peter, I wonder what could have
    done it?
I shrugged my heavy shoulders.
I don't know, she said, whether one can give a piece of machinery
    a proper burial. Might it not be better, she sniggered, to fasten it
    in a memorial clock, so that one always thought of poor Peter as
    one looked at the time?
My eye itched, I rubbed it with my ear.
I suppose he was thrown from his elephant, she said, placing one
    tiny foot in the crook of my trunk, and when they dragged him
    away this piece remained.
I hoisted her to my back.
But I don't want the beastly thing, she cried from the howdah, and
    she flung the clockwork into the swamp.
As we left, I saw it turn into a golden beetle that buzzed off into a
    belt of wild nasturtiums.

She wears the long series of wonder-awakening dresses,
She wears the fishskin cloak,
She wears the gown of pearl with the constellations slashed into its
    dark lining,
She undresses out of the night sky, each night of the year a
    different sky,
She wears altitude dresses and vertigo dresses,
She plucks open the long staircase at the neck with the big buttons
    of bird-skulls in the white dress of sow-thistle.
She has leather britches known to be chimp-skin,
She has combed star-rays into a shaggy night-dress,
She has a bodice of bone-flounces, a turbinal blouse through which
    the air pours.
There is a gown she has that shimmers without slit or seam like the
    wall of an aquarium:
A starfish moves slowly on its pumps across her bosom,
A shark glides, a turtle rows silently between her knees,
And she adopts in turn the long dress of sewn louse-skin,
The romper suit of purple jam packed with tiny oval seeds,
The foggy grey dress, and lapping between its folds
Echo bird-cries and meteor-noises and declarations of love,
The ballgown of ticker-tape,
The evening dress of flexible swirling clockwork running against
    time,
The cocktail dress of bloody smoke and bullet-torn bandages,
And the little black dress of grave-soil that rends and seals as
    she turns.
Often she sits up all night in the philosopher's library
Sewing strong patches from his wardrobes of thought
Into her wounded dresses.

V LEARNING-LADY

I sprained my wrist taking her skirt off; it was moving too fast in a
    contrary direction.
I grasp the difficult mathematics of topology because I know her
    saddle-shapes.
I know conic sections also from the fall of her skirt.
Transcendental numbers are not difficult since inside she is much
    bigger than she is out.
As for theology, she always gives me good answers to my short god.

VI COMING-LADY

She comes like a seashell without a skin,
She comes like warm mud that moves in sections.
She comes with long legs like a tree-frog clambering
Towards some great fruit, niddip, niddip.
A small acrobat lives inside her flower;
The canopy blooms.
She has an underground belfry tolling the bushes
Which shakes the ground,
It is full of shivering bats that fly out and return.
Her blouse comes off like the clean paging of new books,
There is a smell of fresh bread and a clean active
Strong-teated animal inside.
Her knickers come off like opening party invitations,
And between her legs pigeons are laying eggs without shells.
I have lost dread there longer than a man reasonably may,
I believe I know there white lids sledding over mossy wells,
Shearing prisms and silk splitting for me to walk
Into the red room in order to inspect the ancient portraits
In warm loose oils that are always repainting themselves.

TAPESTRY MOTHS

for Vicky Allen

I know a curious moth, that haunts old buildings,
A tapestry moth, I saw it at Hardwick Hall,
'More glass than wall' full of great tapestries laddering
And bleaching in the white light from long windows.
I saw this moth when inspecting one of the cloth pictures
Of a man offering a basket of fresh fruit through a portal
To a ghost with other baskets of lobsters and pheasants nearby
When I was amazed to see some plumage of one of the birds
Suddenly quiver and fly out of the basket
Leaving a bald patch on the tapestry, breaking up as it flew away.
A claw shifted. The ghost's nose escaped. I realised

It was the tapestry moths that ate the colours like the light
Limping over the hangings, voracious cameras,
And reproduced across their wings the great scenes they consumed
Carrying the conceptions of artists away to hang in the woods
Or carried off never to be joined again or packed into microscopic
     eggs
Or to flutter like fragments of old arguments through the unused
     kitchens
Settling on pans and wishing they could eat the glowing copper
The lamb-faced moth with shining amber wool dust-dabbing
     the pane
Flocks of them shirted with tiny fleece and picture wings
The same humble mask flaming in the candle or on the glass bulb
Scorched unwinking, dust-puff, disassembled; a sudden flash among
     the hangings
Like a window catching the sun, it is a flock of moths golden
     from eating
The gold braid of the dress uniforms, it is the rank of the family's
     admirals

Taking wing, they rise
Out of horny amphorae, pliable maggots, wingless they champ
The meadows of fresh salad, the green glowing pilasters
Set with flowing pipes and lines like circuits in green jelly
Later they set in blind moulds all whelked and horny
While the moth-soup inside makes itself lamb-faced in
The inner theatre with its fringed curtains, the long-dressed
Moth with new blank wings struggling over tapestry, drenched
   with its own birth juices

Tapestry enters the owls, the pipistrelles, winged tapestry
That flies from the Hall in the night to the street lamps,
The great unpicturing wings of the nightfeeders on moths
Mute their white cinders . . . and a man,
Selecting a melon from his mellow garden under a far hill, eats,
Wakes in the night to a dream of one offering fresh fruit,
Lobsters and pheasants through a green fluted portal to a ghost.

SERIOUS READERS

All the flies are reading microscopic books;
They hold themselves quite tense and silent
With shoulders hunched, legs splayed out
On the white formica table-top, reading.
With my book I slide into the diner-booth;
They rise and circle and settle again, reading
With hunched corselets. They do not attempt to taste
Before me my fat hamburger-plate, but wait,
Like courteous readers until I put it to one side,
Then taste briefly and resume their tomes
Like reading-stands with horny specs. I
Read as I eat, one fly
Alights on my book, the size of print;
I let it be. Read and let read.

A TWELVEMONTH

In the month called Bride
there is pale spectral honey
and in-laws made of chain-mail and whiskers.

In the month called Hue-and-Cry
green blood falls with a patter
and the pilchard-shoal flinches.

The month called Houseboat
is for conversing by perfume
and raising beer-steins:
great stone-and-foam masks.

In the month called Treasurechest
snails open jalousies onto their vitals:
pinecones, pollen-packed.

In the month called Brickbat
the sea is gorgeous with carpets
of orange jelly-fish squads:
and the people ride.

The month called Meatforest
is for flowers in the abattoirs,
catafalques for the steers.

In the month known as William
we watch the deer grazing on seaweed;
police open the strongroom of Christ.

In the month called Clocks
the poets decide
whether they shall draw salary,

And in the month called Horsewhip
they pluck their secret insurance
from the rotting rafters.

In the Mollycoddle month
barbers put up bearded mirrors
and no-one is allowed to die.

In the month called Yellow Maze
all the teddy-bears
celebrate their thousandth birthday.

In the month called Sleep-with-your-wife
the sea makes a living
along this quiet shore, somehow.

THREE AQUARIUM PORTRAITS

(Penzance)

I

The lobster leans, and taps on the glass.
Among the fiery hands of light and ripple
It has a face like a barbershop of scissors
Shaving drowned men in a lambent steely light;
It has a face and shell
Of blue holly-leaves in a beating-gently breeze;
These details cleaning themselves always
Scissors through combs, and leaf rescrubbing leaf.

It walks like three headless armoured dancers
Of a machinetooled Masque of Industry
Who set their precision clawsteps down
With computed watery stilts on feathery ooze
That sends up gunpuffs. It sees
But it sees through sucked black stones on skinny telescopes.
Its swept-back aerials are the only red instruments.

It is *loppestre*, or spidery creature, but I dub it
Lob's Man, as a teamster gathers up his reins
Lobster has spikes and studs for harnessing to some evil,
Must be the jigsaw piece for some horn-hoof pattern
Being like a witch that marshlight blue
Carrying its hell's radio in those crimson aerials.
There! I can eat it with good conscience
Being our Lob-Star, the colour of Sirius,
Clanking on its platter, alive-boiled and buttered:
We shall eat the evil and make it our very own,
Cracking his male-claws with our silver pincers.

II

This is one picture along the dark corridor
Of windows like a train under the sea.
Instead of scenery streaming, flocks of birds,
We have the fishes who swim their little masks
Of innocence with big dark eyes in silver faces,
Of pouting generalship, decorated fins,
And nibble at her fingers, through the glass.
With ripples, dusky lights, these frames
Seem full, as the passage is, with fiery hands
That push out with other portraits, as
CUTTLEFISH AMONG GLASS-SHRIMPS.

III

The boots have golden eyes, like cats or sheep,
Slashed with a wavery iris, rippling welts.
They blush dark as fruitcake with a chewing beak
Deep in the centre of a flower of tendrils.
There is a creamy wand set in the moccasin
And when they slip upstairs as they like to do
Aiming this waterhose at their launching-pad
They are something between a pussy and a carnival-nose

Something between a fruitcake and a boot
A cross between a miniskirt and a pasty
Float water-gently like a gold-eyed turd
Of inscrutable wisdom among their glassy shrimps
High-stepping like lean assistants who are
Mainly spectacles and the joints of spectacles
Being entirely of glass with a few guts
But shining like a neon sign at every joint
Like ladders who are greenhouses and jobbing gardeners
Who are bees returning also, joints pollen-packed,
Easing their silver slivers like encased decisions
Of see-through steel whose clickering chimes
Bright-sparkle in water-sound, deafened by glass.

Among the always-twitching hands of fire
The creatures watch us, lobster
Ripped spiky from its pattern of imagined evil,
Precision prawns, those workers in glass,
And the biscuit-coloured, jet-propelled
And boot-faced cuttlefish.
They lean and tap the glass, and shiver
As we scratch back. To them
We are as they are, sea-creatures that float
With no support along the fiery corridors.
Through the glass
They wish to eat us, and turn us to themselves,
We lean back at them, our watery mouths
Like smashed aquaria with jagged fangs,
We return each others' looks among fiery hands.

ON LOSING ONE'S BLACK DOG

(An expression meaning 'to reach the menopause')

I

Thigh-deep in black ringlets,
Like a shepherdess at a black sheepshearing;
Like a carpentress in a very dark wood
Sawdust black as spent thunderstorms;
Like a miller's wife of black wheat
The stones choked with soot;
Like a fisherwoman trawling black water
Black shoals in the fiddling moonlight
Squaring with black nets the rounded water;
Like an accountant, knee-deep in black figures,
A good fat black bank balance in credit with grandchildren!
Tadpole of the moon, sculptress of the moon
Chipping the darkness off the white
Sliving the whiteness off the night

Throw down the full gouges and night-stained chisels!

Coughing black
Coughing black
Coughing black

The stained lazy smile of a virgin gathering blackberries.

II

We opened the bungalow.
The sea-sound was stronger in the rooms than on the beach.
Sand had quiffed through the seams of the veranda-windows.
The stars were sewn thicker than salt through the window
Cracked with one black star. A map of Ireland
Had dripped through the roof on to the counterpane

But it was dry. There was no tea in the tin caddy,
Quite bright and heartless with odorous specks.
There was a great hawk-moth in the lavatory pan.
Our bed was the gondola for black maths, and our
Breakfast-table never had brighter marmalade nor browner toast.

Two ladies in a seaside bungalow, our dresses
Thundered round us in the manless sea-wind.
Her day-dress: the throat sonata in the rainbow pavilion.
We kiss like hawk-moths.

III EPHEBE

The beating of his heart
There was no translation

Eyes so round
The lad looked at me milkily

I had his confidence
In the dry street
Out came his secret

'The Battleship,' he said,
'We're going to see the Battleship'

As though a flower told me
Opened its deep pollens to me

He had teeth perfect and little as
Shirtbuttons, fresh and shining

He was about eight
Like a flower grown in milk

'The Battleship!' he said
So lively   supernatural
His soft thumbprint
Creeping among the canines

IV CRY JELLIES AND WINE

Preparing jellies and wines in autumn
Sad wife alone
The rooms golden with late pollen

The neat beds turned down
The children smiling round corners
Sweet-toothed, sweet-headed
Her fruit, her blueberries on canes

The sad wife who would not listen
Boiling jellies, filtering wines in autumn
What shall she tell the children

They will not listen
They love jellies, russet jams

The sad wife in autumn
Her jellies and wines stolen
Stolen by love, stolen by children

The rooms golden with pollen

V A VIBRANT WASP

A wasp hanging among the rose-bines:
Footballer wandering in an antique market;
Damask and ebony, mahogany thorns, greenglass rafters, veined
    parquets.

Again he struck the wasp with the sheets of paper and
Believes he kills it; the wasp
Clinging to the tendon of his ankle looked very sporting and official
In black and gold clinging by the tail the high-pitched pain
Was yellow streaked with black oaths

He could not find the wasp-body it had been sucked
Along his nerves
                        after the rage
There is a sore pain turning to lust

That afternoon a plucky infant was conceived
Full of an infant's rage and juices
He struck once, and conceived

He struck at the wasp once, his child
Ran in out of the garden, bawling like a plucky infant
Teased beyond endurance in a striped football jersey among gigantic
    cronies.

VI THE STATUE OF HER REVERED
BROTHER-IN-THE-BOAT

She catches the bloodless statue of her
Revered boatman-brother a ringing blow with
A mallet; the pure note vibrating
Through the gouged stone sustains
For three hours of morning reverie
During which time at this pitch
(*Om*) her petitions come to pass
Beyond her expectations, or anybody's: gardens, walks,
Silvery lads and encounters among the knotgardens,
Clavichords humming to the shrill-chanting beds
In the manor dark as horn. Too soon
The singing stone falls silent and it is not yet time
To strike the next blow. Now that she has seen everything

It is time to strike the last blow, now that she has
Nothing further to ask, it is time to plead
That the rigid statue may grant its greatest boon and walk
As her living and immortal brother among
All the beds and garden beds and wives and grandchildren
Proved by the magic of her singing jewel; but first
Before he can so walk she must strike some blow,
The ultimate blow, the blow to end all blows

To finish things one way or the other, that will either
Reduce the great icon to bloodless rubble or
Free her brother to return
                              rowing in
From the further shore: either
Make the wishing-stone alive in granting
The goal of bliss, or
                    shatter felicity, all.
                                        (This blow
Is struck only by the lunatic when the moon is
Full and directly overhead and the stony particles
Aligned like the cells of a yearning throat
Ready to sing, the birth-passage of man-song
Through a woman-throat)

In the beginning it was violence only and the shedding of blood
That started the gods singing.

VII AT THE PEAK

The tables laid with snow
Spotless cold napery

Tense white snowmen
Seated on snowthrones
Knives of sharp water
Icepuddle platters

Iceflowers

50

Carving the snowgoose
Slices whiter than pages

The sun rises
The self-drinkers
Swoon under the table,

Glitter the mountain.
The rivers foam like beer-drinkers

Devising real flowers
And meat you can eat.

VIII THE TUTORIAL

My anointing
Gathers him
I draw the shapes of him
He has yet to learn
Over his skin
He recognises them

Flowing from feet to head
Baptism

He is a stony river, he swims with his head on the river
The brown body

I draw wings in the oil along his back
He is a youthful messenger

I anoint his chest
He is one of the facetious learned folk
Silky
It is my learning

I tweak his nipple
The county thunders
White oil
Displaces my
Black mirror.

THE VISIBLE BABY

A large transparent baby like a skeleton in a red tree,
Like a little skeleton in the rootlet-pattern;
He is not of glass, this baby, his flesh is see-through,
Otherwise he is quite the same as any other baby.

I can see the white caterpillar of his milk looping through him,
I can see the pearl-bubble of his wind and stroke it out of him,
I can see his little lungs breathing like pink parks of trees,
I can see his little brain in its glass case like a budding rose;

There are his teeth in his transparent gums like a budding
    hawthorn twig,
His eyes like open poppies follow the light,
His tongue is like a crest of his thumping blood,
His heart like two squirrels one scarlet, one purple
Mating in the canopy of a blood-tree;

His spine like a necklace, all silvery-strung with cartilages,
His handbones like a working-party of white insects,
His nerves like a tree of ice with sunlight shooting through it,

What a closed book bound in wrinkled illustrations his father
    is to him!

PLACE

The train's brakes lowing like a herd of cattle at sunset
As it draws up by Lesson's Stone, by mountains
Like deeply carved curtains, among small birds
Knapping at the stationmaster's crumbs, hopping-black
Like commas of wet ink: I could see their small eyes glisten.
I thought I must die in my sleep, I lay in my bunk
Like wet clothes soaking, the convulsions were the journey,

The bedroom bumped. I stepped off and the mountain landscape
Was like stone guests set round a still table
On which was set stone food, steaming
With the clouds caught on it; a plateau
Surrounded with peaks and set with cairns
And stone houses, and a causeway up to Giant's Table,
And the railway trailing like a bootlace. My house
Was hard by Lesson's Stone, near the sparkling Force
That tumbled off the cliff, that in summer
Left its dry spoor full of thornbush. Then the lizards
Flickered among the rocks, like shadows
Of flying things under a clear sky, or like
Bright enamelled painted rock on rock, until they swiftly
Shot sideways too fast to see. I arrived
On Lesson's Stone Stop platform a decade ago;
The place where I live is still like pieces
Of a shattered star, some parts shining
Too bright to look at, others dead
As old clinker. I am afraid to mention
The star's name. That would set it alight.

A great longhaired hog, glistening with the dew,
It knows night by heart, sucked through blue irises,
But day it allows to rest and glitter on its skin
And its long hairs harsh as fingernails
Like coarse reeds on a hump of the bog.
It is a golden pig and its underslung rod
Is the very word for *thrust*, like the drill
Into the future, and it will run along that drill's sights;
But now, glistening with distillate, it waits
For the sun to raise moulds of steam along its back,
For the sun to warm it dry and the air to towel it
Testing its hooves meanwhile that clock on the stone,
Ready with its seed and tusks and bolts of muscle
And the grease of seed it pumps into the black sow
Like lightning-bolts into the hulking black thunder anvil
And the storm will gather until it breaks and rains pigs,
The mud glorious with rain-shine, pig-grease and wallow.

OR WAS THAT WHEN
I WAS GRASS

I was putting a bandage of cobweb on the sudden cut
In the pain the fly told me what the web was like
The spider's face with its rows of diamond studs
And my skin crackling as the pincers drove in
That crackling pain went all over me
I knew I would never grow well again, my shell crazed,
And the acid came from the jaws and began to turn me liquid
And I felt a terrible pressure all over with the suction
And I was drawn up through the tusks into that face.
Then I woke up as though I were in a distillery
Humming with energy, retorts of horn and transparent tubes
Buzzing with juices, but I was at rest
Sealed like wine in crystal vases, and I looked down myself
With my eyeskin which was the whole egg, and I felt
The wine condense and become smoky and studded with rows
Of the eyes through which I saw that the mother watched
Benevolently from the roof of the factory which was herself
And my father whom she had eaten was with me too
And we were many flies also contributing to the personality
Of the eight-legged workshop, and I began to remember the man

I had fed on as a maggot or was that when I was grass
Or the snail slying from my shell crackled on the thrush's anvil?
And whenever my eyes closed or my shell crackled in pain,
It was as though I stepped out of black winged habits.

SEAN'S DESCRIPTION

The grave of the careless lady who swallowed pips,
From the rich subsoil of her stomach and snapped coffin-timbers
A fine greasy crop of apples glittering

With their waxes; and Sean told me
Over a customary glass the best description he'd read
Of what a dead person looked like, actually:

'A green doughnut with eyeholes in it,' he said,
'A green doughnut with black cream,' as we sat

By the waterlilies rooted in mud of the pub garden,
And a bumble-bee in a tippet of glossy fur
Snatched a line from the air, and I brought
One of her apples from my pocket, and bit
Through the sweet flesh that fizzed with young ciders
And my toothmarks blazed white through the red skin.

'Look,' I said, holding up another firm sweet apple,
'This is what a dead person really looks like; taste her.'

THE WEDDINGS AT
NETHER POWERS

I

The grass-sipping Harvestmen, smelling
Like haylofts on stilts, creaking
Like wet leather; a raven hops
And picks at them through the gravel:
It has macabre dandruff.
In its spotted froth the bark-faced toad squats
Among the daffodils like Stars of David.

II

A wasp crawls over the crucifix, sting out
Searching for a vulnerable part; the savage vicar
Strikes, the usurper bursts in melted butter
And horn-slices; another takes its place
Searching with its sting out over the holy places.

III

A gold-and-black body pinned to a matchstick cross,
The extra leg-pair free, glossy with wax, their cloven
Dancing-pumps shadow-boxing with slow death;
The sting stretched out in agony and clear drops
Slipping along the horny rapier to the tip
Where a woman crops the venom in an acorn-cup.

IV

The laboratory with skylights, the glass assemblies,
Tubes, taps, globes, condensers, flasks and super-hot flames:
With windows wide open to the pouring waterfall
White with every colour and exclaiming with every word,
With roof wide open to the starfall; just down the stream
The Mud Shop, with fifty-seven varieties of bath.

Two birds singing together like learned doctors;
The dew is open on every page;
He washes the dog's feet gently with warm water;
She spreads luminous marmalade on cindered toast;
There is no tree of flies in which creamy skulls lodge, humming,

No dogs here have intercourse with any virgins;
There is a slug in the garden grey as a city kerbstone;
There is a cool sweet book of one page bound in appleskin.

VI

One hundred ship-weddings, the scoured planking, the pure sails,
The bride's train blazing across the scrubbed poop,
The century of marriages and a hundred brides
Pulled over the water by their blinding veils.

ON THE PATIO

A wineglass overflowing with thunderwater
Stands out on the drumming steel table

Among the outcries of the downpour
Feathering chairs and rethundering on the awnings.

How the pellets of water shooting miles
Fly into the glass of swirl, and slop

Over the table's scales of rust
Shining like chained sores,

Because the rain eats everything except the glass
Of spinning water that is clear down here

But purple with rumbling depths above, and this cloud
Is transferring its might into a glass

In which thunder and lightning come to rest,
The cloud crushed into a glass.

Suddenly I dart out into the patio,
Snatch the bright glass up and drain it,

Bang it back down on the thundery steel table for a refill.

MY FATHER'S SPIDER

The spider creaking in its rain-coloured harness
Sparking like a firework. In the cold wind
Round the sharp corner of the house,

In the cold snap of that wind,
Many turned to ice:
Circular icicles.

My father lifted one off
Very carefully over the flat of his glove.
When I see these hedgerow webs

It is always with the sighing of the sea
In my heart's ear; it was at the seaside
In the smell of sand and tar that I first

Understood the universal perfection
Of these carnivorous little crystals
Coiling from their centres like the shells.

They were cruel and beautiful
At the same time; abominable
And delightful; why else did the silly

Flies dart into them to be drunk
Up like horny flasks, as if
The pints of beer had veiny wings –

If I could see those dartboard webs
Surely they could. They are doorways
To death and the mandala-sign

Of renewed and centred life. And this one,
Here, look, with its array of full lenses
(For the thread is fine enough for minutest

Beads to catch and roll the light in strings)
Is like a Washington of the astronomers,
Planned, powerful, radial city, excited by flying things,

At every intersection and along each boulevard
Crowded with lenses gazing upwards, pointing light.

ORCHARD WITH WASPS

The rouged fruits in
The orchard by the waterfall, the bronzed fruits,

The brassy flush on the apples.
He gripped the fruit

And it buzzed like a gong stilled with his fingers
And a wasp flew out with its note

From the gong of sugar and scented rain
All the gongs shining like big rain under the trees

Within the sound of the little waterfall
Like a gash in the apple-flesh of time

Streaming with its juices and bruised.
Such a wasp, so full of sugar

Flew out within the sound
Of the apple-scented waterfall,

Such a gondola of yellow rooms
Striped with black rooms

Fuelled with syrups hovering
At the point of crystal,

Applegenius, loverwasp, scimitar
Of scented air and sugar-energy

Shining up his lamp-tree tall and devious
Given utterly to its transformations

From sharp-scented flowers to honey-gongs,
Giver and taker of pollination-favours,

A small price for such syrups and plunderings,
Its barky flesh, its beckoning fruit,

Its deep odour of cider and withering grasses,
Its brassy bottles and its Aladdin gold-black drunks.

GUNS AND WELLS

I

The artillery-men wait upon the big gun,
They have its banquet piled
And ready in greased pyramids,
They serve the long fat shells like cannelloni,
The gun munches with an explosion.

Molten tears silver our countenances,
Vomit of metal plates the cornfields,
Men blow away like smoke in the ringing brisants.

No doing of mine, says chef-commandant,
I feed the guns only when they are hungry.

She tells me the polished skull of a traitor
Lurks in this well still,
His comrades gave rough justice,
Over the parapet laid his bare neck,
Cutlass-sliced that smuggling head,
Which dropped like a boulder
And is down there to this day, she said,

Polished nearly to nothing,
Bobbing in the well-spring,
Folding and unfolding in the polishing water,
Almost glass, and papery-thin,
Ascending, descending on variable cool water,
Nodding upon a current which is a spine,
Spinning like a film of faintest shadow
Or flexile churchwindow,
Reflating when rain fattens the spring;

Then a sunbeam
Strikes down the brick shaft
And there gazes upwards, revolving in the depths,
A golden face; then the sun

Goes in and the water goes on polishing.

SONG

I chuck my Bible in the parlour fire.
The snake that lives behind the bars there
Sucks at the black book and sweats light;

As they burn together, the codex
Flips its pages over as if reading itself aloud
Memorising its own contents as it ascends curtseying

Like crowds of grey skirts in the chimney-lift,
In particles of soot like liberated print.
The vacant text glows white on pages that are black.

The stars, those illustrious watchers
Arranged in their picture-codes
With their clear heartbeats and their eager reading stares

Watch the guest ascend. Around us in the parlour
The inn-sign creaks like rowlocks.
The drinkers glower as my book burns,

Their brows look black
Like open books that turning thoughts consume.
Then all at once

With a gesture identical and simultaneous
Of reaching through the coat right into the heart
They all bring out their breast-pocket bibles

Like leather coals and pile them in the fire
And as they burn the men begin to sing
With voices sharp and warm as hearth-flames.

The black pads turn their gilded edges and
The winged stories of the angels rise
And all that remains is our gathering's will

Which assembles into song. Each man sings
Something that he has overheard, or learnt,
Some sing in tongues I do not understand,

But one man does not sing. I notice him
As my song takes me with the others. He is
Setting down the words in rapid shorthand

In a small fat pocketbook with gilded edges.

IN THE PHARMACY

for Wendy Taylor

A moth settled on the side of a bottle,
Covering its label, a marvel. The embroidered wings
Of the moth called Wood Leopard. It flutters off

And settles on another bottle. The label of this violet
Fluted container with the glass stopper reads
Lapis invisibilitatis: it would make you disappear.

The moth like a travelling label walks
From bottle to marble bottle with floury wings
Embracing each and tapping with fernleaf tongue

Sugared drops at neck and stopper,
Built like a fat rabbit with gaudy wings extracting
The essence of pharmacies, the compendium,

Staggering from jar to sculptured jar and sealing
Into capsules its own cogitatio,
Implicating in its eggs our explicit medicine.

And the draughts of invisibility, the poisons?
The caterpillar remembers to die, and disappears,
As the labelled stone declares,

All melts to caterpillar soup inside the wrappings
Where the pupa cogitates,
Just the nerve-cord floating like a herring-skeleton,

And round those nerves lovingly unfolds
The nervous wings on which is marked
In beautiful old pharmacy script, the formula.

SHELLS

See shells only as seawater twining back
To the first touch, of seawater on itself;

The water touching itself in a certain way,
With a certain recoil and return, and the mollusc

Starts up in the water, as though the conched wave
Had been struck to stone, yet with the touch

Still enrolled in it, the spot was struck
And life flooded through it

Recording a thin stone pulse of itself,
Its spiral photo-album, its family likeness

Caught in nacreous layers, as if
Your skull grew spiring from a skull-button,

Your roles coiling out of your smallest beginning,
Full of shelves of selves

Turning around each other
Like a white library that has been twisted,

Like a spired library turned in the tornado
Unharmed, keeping the well of itself

Open to past and future,
Full, like the mollusc, of the meat of sense,

The briny meat, twirled by the tornado;
And this, whose fleshy books have swum away,

Emptying the magnificent pearl-building,
All its walls luminous in the sunlight,

Empty stairwell full of sound,
For since the books created the shelves

To fit their message and their likeness,
Echoes of books remain, resounding,

Printed endlessly around the shelving,
Like the seasound of seapages turning over

And over, touching themselves
In a certain way, echoing, reminding,

Evoking new themes of old sea-shapes. A new shell,
A new skull begins again from its speck

Echoing the older books made of water.
See how the clouds coil also above the eggshells of cities,

Touching each other in certain ways, so that
Rain falls; clouds invisible

Over the sea, but when the watery air
Lifts over the land, the white shells float

Crystallised over the hot cities, muttering with thunder.

THE PROPER HALO

In those glad days when I had hair,
I used to love to smarm it down with Brylcreem.
In those old days this was the definition of a boy:
A scowl, Brylcreem, and back pockets, admonished
To refrain from pomades at one's confirmation,
So that the Bishop would not get his hands oiled,
Greasy palms, laying them on. My uncle laughed at me,
And called me 'Horace!' with my flat-combed parting,
My head shining like a boot; though, as a Navy man,
He liked all that sort of thing himself,
Shaking a kind of Bay Rum out of a nozzled bottle
Labelled in Arabic that came from Egypt,
A brick-red Sphinx on yellow sand for scene,
Spidered with Arabic like uncombed hair. Retired,
He would send to London to the importers for it,
And I asked him what the spider-writing meant. He told me:
'If you want to be like Horace, employ our oil.'

When he died, he left me his personal things,
A wristwatch with a back pitted
From tropical sweat, studs and cufflinks
Glorified with tiny diamond-chips, a dressing-case
With hairbrushes useful to me then, his shaving-mirror;
I mourned him, but enjoyed using his things,
Conversing with his shade, taking both parts in the mirror,
Remembering how we talked, fascinated by this grown-up;
And I remembered catching the habit of hairgrease,
He dropping a little in my palm and showing me
How to rub it in with fingertips, 'You'll
Never lose it now, keep up the massage,'
Which wasn't true. Still, when he died
I did have hair, and liked the barber's shop.
A university friend staying with me

Translated the Arabic on the bottle,
Laughing. I said '*What* spirit?' and he said
'Definitely religious advertising; could your uncle
Read the Arabic?' I thought not, though he had
Many spoken phrases. 'Then he picked up "Horace"
From the vendor's gabble; it reads:
"Horus comes to greet you through this oil."'

I liked the barber's shop; the man
Stabs the pointed bottle at his palm;
My dark hair is cut and shaped and forests felled
Over my white-sheathed shoulders lie like toppled pines.
The oil shivers in the barber's palm,
He puts the plump bottle down, and that hand
Descends swooping on the other; they rub together
Like mating birds and as they fly to my head
I see they shine. His rough fingertips
Massage my scalp like the beating of a flock
Of doves; now it is my hair that shines
And stands up as though an ecclesiastical charge
Were passing through me; I laugh! 'You like
The scent of the oil, do you, Sir?' I nod,
Though I don't. It's the shine I love;
I shine with glory! and this is worth
The barber's shillings, many times. I shall feel
Of age as down the street I pass
In my shining pelt and glittering shako, my hair
Cut and shaped like my natural urges, properly, proudly,
In a halo of light and scent, godly contained.

THE FUNERAL

for N.

I

Clouds and mountains were invited, both the conscious
And the unconscious creatures. The trees
Like visible outpourings of the stream's music,
The urine of the animals in the dawn frost
Puffing like rifle-fire. The dark meat of the sun,
The bloody meat, the cremating sun.

II

Ninety-two percent of what we eat is from direct
Pollination by the bees, he tells me this
To cheer me and if true ninety-two percent
Of what he says with his mouth is said by bees. The first light
On leaves shines like apples hanging in the trees,
The whole forest a vast orchard, and all things
Are more than they seem, for they may fly away,
And disappear like Mother pausing on the threshold
Of the fields of light, which are like dew
Thick in the grassy meadows, for the light hangs
Dripping in the leaves, stands on the wind.

III

There is a Witness, I think, who has magnetic wings.
First it seemed to me at the funeral service with the terrible
Useless brass handles that would be saved screwed to
The veneer cardboard coffin which was much too small
That my emotions such as these swirled round my flesh
And some of them spurted from my eyes but ninety-two percent
Were beating in my back in a sensation like spread wings.
Since mine were sprouting I was able to see
The wings of others, such as my father's, standing next to me,

And his were ragged and tattered like those of an old moth
Close to drying up and drifting away, it seemed my duty
To merge my birth-wet wings with his, and this I did,
Entwining them in an embrace with him that he would never know,
And sure enough he, the widower, perked up,
And I felt tattered, but not dry, for back at the house
I sobbed my heart out in the little white-tiled loo,
And there was still a little angelic witness lodged in my spine
At the small of my back, in Jesus-robes, little calm watcher
In white, which I cannot explain, merely report.

IV

The other thing the funeral showed me, unpromising seance,
My Mother, subject of it, at the door ajar
On the field of light, looking back over her shoulder,
Smiling happiness and blessing me, the coherent veil
Of the radiant field humming with bees that lapped the water,
    and she bent
And washed her tired face away with dew and became a spirit.

THE MAN NAMED EAST

The dew, the healing dew, that appears
Like the dream, without warning, hovering on the blades;
The motions of his wings bring dew and light,

The man named East. The ghosts have lost
All sense of perspective
In the drinking-water, twisting and turning,

Shaped by too many vessels, and furrowed
By too many fearful vessels, for we
Drink the water of a drowned village

Of a drowned College from College Reservoir,
And across our drinking-water goes
A small yacht like a lighted kitchen,

A fishing-boat like a ruined cottage,
Dinghies like little violins
With squeaky rowlocks, with violin-voices,

With the devil's music written on the waters.
I stand by the small stream which contributes.
I kneel and dip my hand in, it insists

Into my palm with a slight pressure
Like a baby's hand, which is still
The elasticity of yards of water

Reaching down the hill
From the clouds on high; I crouch
With my hand in that baby's hand

Feeling the slight movement of its fingers,
The light clasp which is love,
The little bony stones rattle

And the cool flesh of glass sinews;
It babbles like a baby, I bend
My ear to the water and now I find

Underspeech I did not hear before;
With the forest like a vast moth
Settling its wings on the hill,

I dip my finger in my mouth and taste
Forests and air and the ice
Of the white rain-wing and its power-pinions.

WARM STONE FOR N

I

Death as pure loss, or immutability.
A watch falling into the well,
Ticking a while in the cool spring, distributing

Its faint shock; or death
As a diamond-second in the year, set
Glittering cold in the anniversary,

The tiny diamond in her ear
Surviving the cremation?

II

Death suddenly appearing, like a spiderweb in the fog,
A piece of paper opening into a house, the snapshot
Through an open door, and at the table sitting still

Somebody; the house
With one room and no kitchen,
The house with the card door;

The disposable house.

III

I turn my back on the ascensions,
The unscreened smokestacks, I do not wish
To watch her ascending, the knots

Solving themselves, fading,
Climbing into the antechambers of rain.
Besides, her smoke should be white,

Blinding!

IV

And the colour of lost rain escaping!
And the photographs white
As the clothes are empty.

I open the prayer-book;
It is empty.

So, with her death,
I will baptise this small
Quartz; it shall stand for death

Like a glass room
Of which only a spirit knows the door,

Which only a spirit can enter
Turning and showing itself in the walls
Lined with warm mirror

Knowing its form in floor and ceiling,
Able to say 'I am here!'

V

It shall become a custom,
Warm room ringed to my finger,
Warm so long as I am warm,
Then left to my daughter

To keep warm, and bequeathed
To hers; warm stone
It will house multitudes.

PNEUMONIA BLOUSES

The iron ships come in with hellish music
They are dedicated to golden oils and engines
And explosive riveting, their hulls heal
To tattoos of guns or iron drums, riveting.
And they worship the horse-mackerel and the sardine,
And why not, it is a living,
And a multitudinous beauty, that brings the souls in.
You see the machine-shop glitter in the tin,
They are water-moths flocking in their thousands;
The packers fit the silver engines in
Laid down in olive oil that is golden;
The key unwinds. Girls
In pneumonia blouses greet the fishermen
Whose balls are brimmed with nitroglycerine of souls,
In each lacy belly the embryo buoyant
As a nenuphar. In the sunlight
The old stone watches sweet and yellow as honeycomb.
Holding the milky child
Is like holding sleep in a bundle,
Which seeps everywhere. There is still frost
In the early morning shadows like spirit-photographs
And like the lace of girls in pneumonia blouses
Ruffled as are the wakes of working boats, fishermen's eyes
Open in all directions, but the shadows of night
Trawl them back again, the nets
Invisible in the black water.

HORSE LOOKING OVER DRYSTONE WALL

for S.C.

A horse dips his nose into dry shadow
Gathered in the chinks like water.
He drinks the coastal dark
That dwells behind the wallstones
In the dry boulder caverns.

Light lies along his muzzle like a stone sheath.
From skull-darkness kin to the dry stone wall
The eyes watch like mirrors of stone;
This horse is half light, half dark,
Half flesh and half stone
Resting his silver muzzle on the shadowed wall
Like a horse made partly of the silver of clouds,

And partly it is a boulder with mane and nostrils
Watching over his wall the plentiful wild boulders
Maned with shaggy weed in galloping water which are kin,

Coralled boulders nostrilling under their manes and lathered
    with brine.

In the Hall of Saurians, the light worked the bones,
The shadows stamped. I was haunted
With the heads colossal in death.
My father brought me here
In his bright shadowless car,
His jewel which he drives everywhere
As a coffin is lined in white satin
Brilliant in the darkness, like mother of pearl.

The wall of the Insect Gallery is splashed
In a butterfly shape with all the British Lepidoptera
And there are five times as many moths shown
For the Shadow in these times
Is correspondingly more significant than the Light.
What goes on in the darkness sees by perfume.
They say that to go out in the noon
Is to lose one's shadow,
To lose the moth of oneself.

My seed, my moth, was torn from me
Like gossamer in the wind
By the lady curator of all these bones,
Mistress of the Halls of Patterns of Death,
Keeper of the probable forms,
The underworld that is delivering constantly
The forms of life, at night like mud
That is a turreted museum, with endless galleries,
But at dawn, nevertheless,
The rainbow glides closer to us across the water
Until we stand within its coloured shells,
Its sequent halls. This is our form
Of transport, the ecstasy of these halls,

The forms displayed. My father in his jewel
Scurries away among the beetles.
The corpse of London transforms in his mouth,
His tales make of it a winged thing
Full of custom and surprise.
But these are winged buildings
As we make love after hours
In the Hall of the Saurians, and the flickering light
Works the bones and the shadows stomp
As up to a campfire smoky with jungle moths
To warm themselves or crush it out.

AT THE COSH-SHOP

Hard rubber in its silk sheath like a nightie:
The assistant offered me a small equaliser,

A Soho Lawyer that could be holstered
In a specially-tailored back pocket,

And he would introduce me to his friend
The trouser-maker. I did not think this

Necessary, but I asked, Why the silk?
It seemed luxurious for such a hard argument.

Oh, Sir, so that it will draw no blood!
He seemed surprised I asked; I thought this not right;

I believe it was the blackness
The makers did not like to show,

Like an executioner it should draw on
Lily gloves, or like a catering waiter

For an instrument that performs a religious service,
Letting the ghost out temporarily with a shriek:

While all is peace within
They steal your worldly goods

Settling the argument by appeal
To deep non-consciousness

With a swift side-swipe, the Bejasus out of him –
Or an act of sexuality, equivalent?

Do the same people make the instrument
That will put the Bejasus back into a person?

The silk then would be the finest, for silk chafing
Hard rubber rouses electricity, it would be

Moulded to the individual sculpt of her lover,
Providing wisely for a longish trip, could seem

Dressed in his silk pyjamas, hard and tingling,
Or as the white silky cloud conceals the thunder

And the black current
That is going to shoot its white darts up and through.

INTO THE ROTHKO INSTALLATION

(Tate Gallery, London)

Dipping into the Tate
As with the bucket of oneself into a well
Of colour and odour, to smell the pictures
And the people steaming in front of the pictures,
To sniff up the odours of the colours, which are
The fragrances of people excited by the pictures;
As the pair walk down the gallery
On each side of them the Turners glow
As though they both were carrying radiance
In a lantern whose rays filled the hall like wings
That brushed the images, which glowed;

Into the Installation, which smells
Of lacquered canvas soaking up all fragrance,
Of cold stone, and her scent falters
Like cloth torn in front of the Rothkos
Which are the after-images of a door slammed
So blinding-white the artist must shut his eyes
And paint the colours floating in his darkness.

He chose the darkest of the images for that white,
That green; red on red beating to the point
Where the eye gasps, and gives up its perfume
Like a night-flowering plant; and with many
Thin washes he achieves the effect
Of a hidden light source which smells
Like water far off in the night, the eye
So parched; paintings you almost can't see;
As if in painting
The Israelites crossing the Red Sea
He painted the whole wall red, and,

Black on black therein,
God somewhat like a lintel. We brought
The lanterns of ourselves in here
And your imagination blotted our light up, Rothko;
The black reached out, quenching our perfume
As in a dark chapel, dark with torn pall,
And our eyes were lead, sinking
Into that darkness all humans have for company;

Standing there, eyes wide, her lids faltered
And closed, and 'I see it, now' she said
And in her breath a wonderful blaze
Of colour of her self-smell
Where she saw that spirit-brightness
Of a door slammed open, and a certain green insertion
Shifting as her gaze searched
What seemed like a meadow through the white door
Made of lightning, cloud or flowers, like Venusberg
Opening white portals in the green mountain
Stuffed with light, he having used
The darkest of all that spectrum almost to blindness

And in his studio in the thin chalk of dawn
Having passed inwardly through that blackness,
Slitting his wrists, by process of red on red
He entered the chapel under the haunted mound
Where the white lightning of another world
Flashed, and built pillars. We left
The gallery of pictures rocked
By the perfume of a slammed eye, its corridors
Were wreathed with the detonation of all its pictures
In the quick of the eye, delighting into
Perfumes like fresh halls of crowded festival.

PLAYING DEAD

His dead-white face,
The eyelids of chalk
With the bold black cross marked

Cancelling the eyes, declaring
Hollow-socketed death, and the
Marble-white countenance

Declaring death
And the red nose to admit
He had died drinking

And the vertical eyelid-stripe
Telling us not only can he open
His eyes up and down but also

From side to side in the stare
Of a real ghost
Who does as he likes

Because Death breaks all the rules, and is
At very best an outrageous joke, and almost
Whatever Death does is quite soon forgotten;

So the Clown pratfalls on the skeleton
Of a banana, and two well-dressed Clowns
Accelerate with custard pies their mutual putrefaction,

As if it were funny to worry overmuch
About these bodies we wear like increasingly
Baggy pants with enormous knucklebuttons, especially
If like that sepulchral makeup they wipe off
In cold cream to white sheer speechless laughter.

THE BIG SLEEP

Sea, great sleepy
Syrup easing round the point, toiling
In two dials, like cogs

Of an immense sea-clock,
One roping in, the other out.
Salt honey, restless in its comb,

Ever-living, moving, salt sleep,
Sandy like the grains at eyes' corners
Of waking, or sleepiness, or ever-sleeping;

And when the sun shines, visited as by bees
Of the sun that glitter, and hum in every wave,
As though the honey collected the bees;

The honey that was before all flowers, sleepiness,
Deep gulfs of it, more of it than anything,
Except sleepy warm rock in the earth centre

Turning over slowly, creating magnetism,
Which is a kind of sleepiness, drowsy glue
Binding the fingers, weakly waking fingers,

Or fingers twitching lightly with the tides;
And the giant clock glides like portals, tics
Like eyelids of giants sleeping, and we lie

In Falmouth like many in a bed,
And when the big one turns
We all turn; some of us

Fall out of bed into the deep soil,
Our bones twitch to the tides,
Laid in their magnetic pattern, our waters

Rise like white spirits distilled by the moon,
Can get no further, and turn over
Heavy as honey into the sea

To sleep and dream, and when the big one dreams
We all dream. And when she storms
We all weep and ache, and some fall

Into her gulfs as she tosses, and we weep
For the lifeboats toiling on the nightmares . . .
But in those beds waters touch each other

Coiling, in a certain way, and where they touch,
At the very point, a mineral spark,
A bone begins to grow, someone is

Putting bones together in the gulf,
In her accustomed patterns – and in their season
The women walk about the town, a big drop

Of the Dreamer in their bellies, and in the drop
A smaller dreamer, image of themselves,
Who are the image dreamed by the ocean's drop,

By the two clocks, one roping in, one out.

BELLS

Bells, the men are mending
The broken church-bells
In the silent church
Silent as a hollow cliff,
They clamber in linen-covered boots
Up and down the bells' mountains,
The chafing of their clambering boots
Produces from all the bells
A low sweet humming,
From the serious shape of bells
Their sound-look of sorrow
Like a tear swinging and crying
Crying and never falling;
The church with its note
That must be charged by bells,
Nave-tone that gathers
Gradually into audibility
Like a singing, and falls
Below the threshold of hearing

Unless it is rung and charged
By bells with true notes
And men with the changes right;
That prolongs the singing.
The men are repairing them.
Buds like birds sit perched
With tightly-folded wings,
The bush is like a silent church
Ready to sound.
In the cliff a great door of sunshine
Swings open and closes again
As the clouds scud: ice-grey chalk
Flooding with gold.

It is full of tuned chambers that are tiny shells
With ancient frosty tones, it is a milliard church,
And a flood-lit skull that goes dark;
A chalkface mirror
To sunshine, like a moon on earth; the child
Stands a moment in its light
And walks away inspired;
In the sun's heat
The crystals of chalk, the tiny fossils
In their billions
Have given off a tone
Like a bell mended by the sunlight.
The quarry nearby
Bears the open wound of the church
Ripped from its flank, in negative.

THUNDER-AND-LIGHTNING POLKA

to J. H. Barclay

The fishmonger staring at the brass band
Offers us golden eyes from a cold slab
And silver instances of sea-flow. The birds

Which were dinosaurs once blanco the stone hats
Of pale admirals. The bandsmen puff their looping brass,
The music skating round and round its rinks

Of shiny tin, the hot trombones and the cool
And silvery horns, light
Sliding like the music along these pipes

And valves, curlicues and flaring tunnels,
Shells, instances of sonorous
Air-flow; we take a piece and present it

On the cold air to the staring ears
Of the sea fishmonger with his wet pets, our part
Of the hypersensitive cabaret. The river

Slides past all the feet; opal mud
Full of sunshine, some dead eye
Caresses the watery catacomb. A hot

Mailed fish has greased windows in the paper,
We eat to music. Above,
A cool high mountain of piled snow,

Its halls stuffed with thunderwork like wardrobes
Of black schoolmasters' gowns and lightning-canes,
White-painted; it turns to one immense

Black gown full of a booming voice from empty sleeves,
And shakes, and shakes its rain down,
And I kiss the thunder-water still booming in every drop

That strikes my face, I hear its flashing brass.
The bandsmen play on in their pavilion,
The instruments flash with lightning,

Their music is full of rain, and fate. I will not go indoors,
My sleeves are wet and heavy
Like velveteen; the trees are shaggy

With birds and lichen, singing in the leaves
In light tones and falling drops that break again
Like little thunder, and cold rain streams across

The wide golden eyes staring from the white slab.

A SCARECROW

A scarecrow in the field,
Dressed like a King
In streamers of tinfoil
Which flash in the sun
And glitter;

And in the deep night
As the moon rises
That glittering again
Appears in the field
As if a fountain
Were standing guard
Over the furrows;

A tattering robe
Of strips of tinfoil
Ragged and gorgeous because
Of its liquid facility with the light,
And so multiplex

That it is a squadron riding
With swords out saluting the light.

The birds rejoice with their song
At this wonder of the sun
Willowing on its cross-pole,
And in this presence of the moon
Raggedy in the fertile field,
And nip therefore their share only
Of seeds sown out of the loam,
And do not multiply their kind
Desperately being content seemingly
That an alchemical balance has been achieved:

The tinfoil rebus in the open field.
Even the vicar, passing the scarecrow field
Is reminded of life
That is not only dust to dust
But light to light and air to air,
Shooting his cuffs,
Flashing his watch.

DRY PARROT

The Parrot of Warlock's Wood,
Of Peter's Wood,
It leaves wide twiggy footprints,
It walks in its cinder wings
Like a tight-buttoned fellow
In oyster-grey tailcoat;

A Parrot has no blood
Only calcium filings,
It dries a room;
Peter keeps the Parrot
To dry the house out;
It was a clinker egg
Before it was a thirsty Parrot.

Now it taps on the clear dry mirror
And with its beak begins
To loosen the mummy plumage
And shake the egg-sand out
And utters an Egyptian cry and flies
Taking to the air up the chimney
Like a roaring hearth-fire
In its anhydrous glory.

THE FIRST EARTHQUAKE

The birds squabbled and fell silent
In their million trees like colleges of monks
With their mean little ways and their beautiful songs;

The yachts like moored forests,
The yachts rocked in their haven
Like women in long dresses

And invisible feet
Bowing to the earthquake.
The mist had rolled in

And developed all the spiderwebs,
The trees in the groves draped
Like pearl-sewn yachts,

The million spiders in them asleep,
The spiders in their white roofs,
The dew-lapping spiders,

They nodded their toolchest faces,
Beards wet with dew,
Dew brimming their webs and their claws;

Complex water shivered everywhere like a single ghost.
Lovers, smelling of almonds and new bread,
Roused from their beds, pointed

Rubbing their eyes at the copses of yachts
That tugged at the tremor and dipped,
Shivering rain from their tackles,

Lovers who shivered like silk
As the rafters groaned
Within their white ceilings,

This earthquake shoved up fifty new fountains!
After the first shock we are ravenous,
The little silvery fishes grizzling in the shiny pans.

THE DYNAMITE DOCTORS

The dynamite doctors
At the explosives factory
They nurse the melted stew

Like greasy gravy or mutton tallow,
A grey potency in its bowls
That must never be stirred too fast

Or else the door opens on a star
Opens on a sun, on creation
And the fire-blast hurries in

Like an angel of death with hair burning.
The ticklish doctors
Skimming the bowls

Tilting them over the kieselguhr
To contrive that virile mud
Called dynamite,

The precious stream that must not break
In its droplets like a stick of bombs,
Otherwise the medicine will suffer an attack

Which will take everyone with it.
One doctor takes the pulse
Of the machine and turns it down

A little, the vibration is excessive;
He dips his finger slowly
Into the gluten and sucks it most gently

So his head shall not explode:
He nods, he must not shake his head.

AT HOME

The spider combs her beard.
One gave me cobweb-pills for the shakes.
There is a black Rasputin-fly that can't be killed,

There is a dustbin boiling with its worms;
My mother scrapes more porridge into the faces.
The flies buzz with swollen lips,

In a Russian, in the translating sunshine.
Dew scuttles down the panes
Like the shaky ghosts of crippled spiders.

I try to rub the glass free and clear
But they are running their races
On the further surfaces. The dry spider

Will raise the wet flies and drink out of them,
Like Bellarmine jugs, like horny flasks
That have wings and faces. Convolvulus

That smells of nice blancmange
Twirls about the dustbin lattice.
My father rushes through the kitchen

Flapping a tea-towel, ushering a ghost of flies
Out of the kitchen into the cool green lane.
There are still flies that circle stolidly

Keeping the pattern just below the ceiling.
They pass through my father's cloth, evidently,
Like spirits of the pattern. He returns.

II

He returns wiping his brow spiderous with dew
And breathing heavily. He shakes his fist
At the immovable fly-pattern round and round the lamp;

My father hefts a shuddering pail of water
And turns it into milk with disinfectant.
He pours it in the choiring bin of maggots.

Their smell of coconut and pus
Fades behind the blanket of hospital pine.
The maggots skip in their stringy boiling.

My mother folds her arms and nods her head.
We settle once more round the breakfast-table,
There is a baby brother hoisted in a high-chair.

The silent changeling grasps the shaggy rusk.
He was born in a smell of pine-needles and maggots.
I was not allowed inside the curtained room.

Its shadows were odorous, and deeper than a cave.
The doctor brisked the taps to scrub his paws.
He smelled of her, and the nurse smelled;

Pine and maggots. In the cave of bedroom shade
Where she has gone, her voice deepens like a man's
Then shatters, and another voice

Lifts in something which is not a song,
And she returns,
Gripping a maggoty bundle, not the same.

This terrible head suited her as well,
Distilling tears and wax and drool,
Lying across the pillow stained like brown paper,

Stamped and water-marked with sweat,
Just unwrapped, this parcel, on a fresh head,
The ginger hair in feeble ringlets,

The mauve lipstick, the broken veins in the cheeks,
Severed at the seamy sheet. It
Begins tossing, lets out an accustomed cry;

I start back, and clamber under the bed.
Here there are long lattices of dust
Rolled up against the wainscot from the blankets,

Fibres minutely ground through the springs
That coil above me, the mill
Of nightmare sickness and copulation,

The flour of germs and fibres rubbed
From bar and dance-hall all loafed together
In long limbless clooties which drift at me,

Shift very slightly in the mattress-wind
That puffs as she turns over in her sleep
Of the medicine alcohols that net her dreams

Blackening in the broken veins
Exhaling tinctures into the fresh window air
That begins again to smell of pine and coconut

And taint her appeaseless, helpless ghost.
It is in the boards and bricks.
The room and house will always smell of it.

UNDERTAKER'S WIND

I

Someone was climbing the pepper-tree;
We let them.
The fig-tree grew out of the cellar;
We let it.

II

The knife used as a book-mark,
The slender knife light,
The book weighty;
In the gutter of the book
Ancient headlines
'Spiritualist Murders Bride';
This tree climbs about our minds.

III

The massive odour of sex
About the whole house,
Building its own sliding casements,
Its doors swinging in the breeze.

The unrefreshing East Wind
Stunting the trees;
It is like a breeze in reverse,
It is a suction
Like the kiss of a man
A spiritualist maybe
Starved for bodies,
Yearning for his bride.

It is a wind with mouths in it.

It is the ambience of the East Wind
Which knocks the wasps down,
One had mistaken her beer
For its paper nest in the amber city which hums,
Going for the gleam in the beer
Went for its rest in her alcohol,
The angry wasp;
She bent over it amused and appalled
'How shall we rescue it?'
Fishing at it with a wooden pencil;
I threw the beer down on the stone paving
Parched by the East Wind

Which sucked the infusion dry,
The wasp glued by its wings
To the fizzing stone.
I stamped on it,
Smeared its appearance across the paving
Like a drawing or a fossil;
'How could you have done it!'
Blood from her steak had stained her creamed potatoes;
'It was the East Wind,' I explained.

V

'The eager wasp that nips for its steak
Small stained loaves of the butcher's bloody sawdust,
That secateurs threads each autumn from my muslin shirt,
Each autumn nibbles from your Shakespeare . . .'

'If you had swallowed it . . .
It would have been like cutting your hand on the book,
Like swallowing the whole pepper-tree,
Like devouring the Undertaker's Wind.'

JOY GORDON

The death of my mother, it
Doesn't mean she's gone for ever,
It means she has crossed over;
I cry because I have tears, and there seems to be
A joy in the air (she liked
To call herself Joy, it was her
Dancing name, Joy Gordon, thus,
When she danced she was my Father's Joy;
His name was Gordon.)

What are ghosts? The medium said
Whenever you think of her,
Greet that image kindly, say
'I'm glad to see you' it will give
The spirit Joy; to be fluxile
Like air, but
Constant as metal,
Not keeping to the one world,
Seeking unity with the living:
I see her now, she dances,
I am very glad to see you dancing,
Joy.

I see spirits, and try
To greet them kindly; and there is never
A company of the living
Without its spirits mingling:
There they were
Doing their Tai Chi
Under the dawn trees, the living
In their loose linen jackets and white ghost-trousers
A ballet of clowns moving as the trees move
To the dawn wind and the dawn chorus,
And among them, spirits,
Like air coiling, as though

Certain enhancing lenses had swept
In front of trees
Or between the dancers;

Under the dawn trees collecting
All the natural forces that do us good,
Gathering the metals of the trees
In manual alchemy, in sequent poses
Adopting the shapes of the vessels
Of human distillation, the hushed
Receptacles, and without, within,
The condensation of a magical dew;
To gather Joy.

The fair-haired one in the long skirt
A portion of the gnosis
Dancing slowly under the dawn trees,
She was the first one there, she was dancing
When I arrived, slowly under the dawn trees
To catch their bright metal, the distillation vessel
Itself dancing.

Just so might my daughter
Call herself Zoe Peters
For dancing or other joys
And signify 'Peter's Life':

I went to fetch her
From a friend's birthday party
In the long upper room of the Church Hall;
Some eleven-year-old lingerers were murdering
'Happy Birthday' on the old piano by the little platform;
There was a memento of iced cake in a twist of polythene
To take home, and there had been dancing;

There was still dancing,
The room was full of dancing, no girls were dancing,
There was dancing up to the ceiling, the air still paced
With Joy and I looked up and greeted them kindly.

THE SMALL EARTHQUAKE

The birds can't soar because all the breath
That carries them has been withdrawn
Into this great hush, the sea and sky

Calm as two mirrors endlessly reflecting.
Then the stars flicker like candles where a door
Is opened, and closed, and the ground

Bumps slowly, like a ferry as it is steered
Into the quay, bumps on its rope fenders;
And afterwards you cannot believe

The ground shifted; except, high up in the corner
Near the ceiling the white has cracked like a web
Until you try to smear it away: the spider

Under the earth spun it and threw it
Into the house; and I recollect a certain
Tang passed through the air, like

A champagne elixir passing from the abyss, creating
A freshet that soaked the grass, a web-crack,
And a jammed window in Zoe's room upstairs.

UNDER THE RESERVOIR

The reservoir great as the weight
Of a black sun radiates through the cracks
In the concrete, expresses water supercharged

By pressure and darkness, the whole body
Of water leaning on the hairline cracks,
Water pumping itself through masonry

Like light through glass. Water charged
By the mystery of lying there in storeys
In transparent tons staring both upwards and downwards

(His coffee hand spills on his shirt the regalia
Of his worried mind in linked splashes like medals
Of a muddy war)

The reservoirs in their unending battle to flow
Turned into steely strain like hammered pewter
Endure their thousand tons of mud, as though

They held their surfaces open like Samson
To the dust that sifts on to their cold pewter,
And rejoice in their dark linings, as they might

Rejoice in plentiful seed,
Black seed of illimitable forest cracking
Open the stone rooms when the water has gone.

FALMOUTH CLOUDS

I

The weather, opening and closing
Doors in the head,

Opening them gently like
A gradual suffusion of sun, or
Slamming thunder-splattered doors shut,

II

With a jangle of chains disclosing
A writhing chain-locker of cloud
Slithering away into itself.

III

A chalky bust of Beethoven breaks open
On rows of ruffled theatre-chocolates which gleam
In the lightning; then, the stars
Walking in long chiffons of rain

IV

Where later chiffons are unrolled
Along a blue counter, a bolt of silk thumped down
So it unrolls with an astonishing perfume
And a blaze of white.

V

In the high wind implosions of dark-cloaked cloud
As through the stage trapdoors called 'vampires', plunge.

VI

An exploding herb-garden or laboratory
Shoots across the sky,
Arrests one's head and simultaneously
Across the inside of that dome
Plants horticultures of changeable perfumes.

VII

That ice-cathedral which built itself from nothing
But faith, is being shot from a cannon
For charity, with silver candlesticks and sonorous arches
And clergy scattering in their whitest surplices;

VIII

The cathedral was full of dazzling tablecloths
Which come rolling everywhere above on which are thrown
Dark shadows from much higher, of personages who appear
To be eating supper at a long table in an upper room.

IX

These clouds are packed with white gulls, while those
Are an aviary of dark rainbirds; when they collide
There is suddenly nothing but sun, hey presto.

X

Skywalkers with immense tension of presence
And extreme visibility and invisibility as well,
The cascades roll past, turn dragonish and then
They are all simple lace very high
On a blue robe which darkens with emergency generating stations
Black as floating mines of coal.

XI

I wake from a dream of crowned and grimacing white faces
To my bedroom window which crowds with vast white faces
    grimacing.

THE TOWN ALTERS SO THE GUIDES
ARE USELESS

I

Roomy white houses, pokey cafes,
Seawaves crisping in, smelling
Of receding storms, the beds
Everywhere of craftsman flowers,
Britain in Bloom, by their rude openings
Showing their craft of perfume,

The craft of perfume and electricity
Which is the town's name,
Its roots deep in the mines.

II

An old mine collapsing at midnight
Drives down the street like a furrowing earthquake;

Like marsh-bubbles of midnight
Mines rise through the houses
As the houses fall;

The airing-cupboard opens on a gritty precipice,
Your shirts fall into the unlaundered blackness
Scented with arsenic and mouldy copperas.

III

Even the trees are falling into the mines,
The woods are falling into the little hills
Which have such great undergrounds;
Even the trees that cure
By the continual utterance
Of their name-sound along the winds
And their perfume on the wind,
Even such trees fall as the hills open;

Even the healing tree
Which drew arsenious oxide up
And broadcast it in homoeopathic amounts,
Even this now descends
To its great white mother-lode in the dark.

Instead of hills
We are left with domes and whistling crags,
Ragged declivities as full of holes
As iron cheeses, copper cheeses.

IV

With delicacy and respect, our lamps lit,
We enter a broad gallery root-roofed
Half a mile down; our leader holds up his hand:
'Hush,' he says, 'do you smell that?'

So we turn our carbide lamps off, can better
Hear the water, and we dare
The bend of the corridor to where
The descended forests are glowing with fruit, in their
    orchard-caverns,
In all the hues of copper, tin and iron; he enters,

Our leader tastes a bronze apple, pronounces it good.

THE SECRET EXAMINATION

The wooden desks, the wooden stools
Inscribed with their flow. The examinees

Inscribe their flow. The invigilator
Has a special smell, kindly snapper;

The examinees smell of a good wash
And clean ironing with no black marks;

There is a lean smell of cream and treacle,
Or, as the Bible says, of milk and honey,

For the examination is going well
And distilling by its queries passionless thought

In small puffs from the alembics
Of sleeves and collars

With the tiny writing motions
And slight nods of head; everybody

In this well-lighted room
Of sharp pencils and dazzling pages

And cleanest clothes is exhaling subtexts,
Is inhaling information secretly colluding;

The invigilator knows there is no copying –
But how can all the answers be identical?

He is suspicious of the brightest boy
And the dullest, equally.

BLACKTHORN WINTER

A blackthorn winter. The trees lighter
Than at other times, showing
The inwards of their leaves; the stars
Because of the bitter wind
Twinkle fiercely; the masses of air
Create a hollow echoing in the woodland;
Sunset's slant light rebuilds ghost villages, echoing
In their shadow-plane out of moist deep foundations,
And celtic boundaries pulse in ceaseless wind-markings;

To smell the touch of the wind, to hear the contours.

SNIFFING TOM

One who goes to and fro in summer
Sniffing the saddles of girls' cycles:
A Sniffing Tom.

The same chap (I know him well)
Farts in the bath and bites the bubbles:
He doubles as a *Snorkist.*

To secure his rank, the prince
Catches in his mouth the rank breath
Of the dying king: this is the *Air Apparent.*

He is crowned soon enough
And married with Holy Rites, which should
More properly be called *Holy Ruts,*

For after copulation the rank dream comes,
And he that dreams also sweats, farts, snores
And erects and should *revere*

Le rêve, its reverie, for he has dreamed
A classy one, that he unlocked
The school shed among the daffodils

And it contained 100 girls' cycles,
So he sleeps to dream again, and sweats,
And he is juicy; that is, *sapient;*

By Jiminy, this is sooth! by the twins
Of the two worlds, soothe, sleep
And wake; *by Gemini!*

IN THE LAB WITH THE LADY DOCTOR

The Old Woman resembles a fairy-tale princess
Who has stayed too long in her tower unrescued,
She precedes me among the benches, she puts
Her protective goggles on, and in this mood
Resembles that gnome who captured me; I look closer:
It is that gnome. She comes in again
With a flock of young men in white flapping coats
To whom she is goosegirl. I insist that the chemicals
On this side of the bench are strictly mine, and this includes .
The bottle of gold salts, and the retort distilling
An infusion of bull-semen. There will be a fight, it's plain,
One of the young Privatdocents has his white coat off already
Underneath which he is naked, and in mock compliment I
  reach out
And shake him firmly by the wedding-muscle, upon which
He hits me all over maybe sixty times
In five seconds with karate blows, one of which
Catches me near my Person but safely thuds
On pubic bone, and I declare 'This assault should not
Have helped your case, but nevertheless this does not mean
That certain experiments cannot be performed in joint names . . .'
At my resolve, a spattering of applause, and the Old Girl
Crosses over from her young squires in dazzling plumage
And asks to see the bruises, so I strip off my shirt.
The marks of striking hands patter across my chest
And already the dark bruises are rainbowing like pieces
Of peacock tail. The young chap who inflicted them
Stands by, sniffing my retort's nozzle; with a shyly winning smile
'Will you give me a drink of this?' he asks. I feel like a fruit
Which has been bruised in order to ferment
Some delicious rare liquor; I say so; they applaud again.

EIGHT PARENTS

I

At the climax of the illuminated
Book of Hours the Trinity is seen in truth to be
Three self-same white-clad bearded figures
Of Jesus on three identical thrones.
It makes the eyes go funny, like trifocals.

II

This devotional picture resembles
My mother's triptych dressing-table mirror;
When she sat there, three other mothers appeared.

III

The fourth turned round to me and smiled;
The three simultaneously looked back over their shoulders
At somebody out of sight down the glass corridors.
Then she got up, and the thrones were empty.

IV

Nearly a decade after she had emptied her throne, my father
Sat himself down in front of the same mirror and died.
He paid his Access- and paper-bill, laid out
Like hands of cards folders on the dining-room table
For his executors, climbed the stairs to his widower bedroom,
Sat down at my mother's mirror and saw there were three
    more of him,
Then his heart burst and shot him into mirror-land.

V

Where is that mirror now? you may be reasonably sure
If you buy a second-hand house or bed, then
Somebody has died in it.

VI

But a dressing-table triple mirror? Can you
Enquire of the vendor, expecting nothing but the truth,
'Who died in this mirror?' Death
Leaves no mark on the glass.

A PASSING CLOUD

I

They tell of thunder picked up on the teeth,
Or radio decoded on a filling, one's mouth
Buffeted with Sousa; but this was a dull ache
Pouring from a black cloud, I could get
No message from this broadcast, I must have
This radio pulled. 'No,' said my father,
'Keep your tooth, this is but a passing cloud.' I knew
It was him, because that was the brand
Of cigarettes he smoked, 'Passing Cloud' by Wills, and
'Yes,' he said abruptly, 'It's me,' and turned white;
By this token I knew he was dead,
Knew it again.

II

When I had flu I always sweated his smell; his two
    wardrobes
Were exhaling it from hanging woollen shoulders like a
    last breath,
This ancient eighty-four-year-old sandalwood was his
    presence now,
It soaked into me and travelled home and stayed some
    days,
Grief like flu; but I could close my eyes and use it as an
    Inn
To meet up with this wayfarer and imagine him.

III

The cat's way is to spray
And then rub her head in the odour
Like a beautiful woman admiring her mirror-image,
Her portrait thick-painted in impasto pheromones;
This is a cat of magic and she lives

In smell-spirit land as the makers of De Retzke
Printing a black cat on their packets, understand.
That was the other brand he used to smoke
Spraying the tinted air like ostrich feathers,
A chieftain's nose of nostril-plumes,
A rainmaker's cloud he passed, admiring
The sensation in the mirror of the smoke,
The sooth-ing oracle and breaker of time,
The redolent satisfaction that snaps the chain
Into peace and the smell of him
Smoking somewhere quietly in the house.

IV

His presence fills the house when he is smoking,
His nature reaches into every cranny,
Into the carpets and eiderdowns and squads of suits;
The chain is broken now, finis,
And though I can smoke in his house now without consent
The smell of cigarettes does not bring him back,
As he is ashes and has been smoked and stubbed out
'A passing cloud . . .' so that time
For him never forges chains again.

V

Except I notice that being under the weather
I sniff my hand-back and his scent appears; my whole skin
And atmosphere remembers him, the rain falls
And my toothache turns to tears, while the world fills
With reflecting mirror-water fathered out of rain-smells.

BLACK BONES

That is a human skeleton under the cataract,
The jet bones shining in the white noise,
The black bones of a man of light;

It is a cascade that accepts
Human form from the bones
That have walked into it, and stand;

It must have been his method of death
To walk into a waterfall and be washed away,
Licked clean down to the jetting bones;

And the bones articulate the roar
Of the cataract that seems to speak
Out of the ribs and skull:

His white-haired sermon from the pelting brow,
The unfathomable water-lidded sockets;
Clad in robes that are foam-opulent,

And never the same clothes twice.

MY FATHER'S TRAPDOORS

Father led me behind some mail-bags
On Paddington Station, my grief was intense,
I was a vase of flowing tears with mirror-walls,

He wore a hard white collar and a tight school tie
And a bristly moustache which is now ashes
And he took me behind the newsprint to kiss me hard,

The travelling schoolboy,
And his kiss was hungry and a total surprise.
Was it the son? Was it the uniform?

It was not the person, who did not belong
Not to father, no.

II

He drove a hole-in-one. It flew
Magnetised into its socket. He'd rummy out
While all the rest shuffled clubs from hearts.
He won always a certain sum on holiday

At any casino; called it his 'commission'.
He could palm cards like a professional.
He had a sideboard of cups for everything

From golf and tennis to public speaking.
He took me to magic shows where people
Disappeared and reappeared through star-studded

Cabinets with dark doors, and magicians
Chased each other through disappearance after disappearance.
He sat down in front of my dead mother's mirror

And disappeared himself, leaving
Only material for a funeral.

III

I looked behind the dressing-table
Among the clooties of fluff and the dust,
I looked under the bed and in the wardrobe

Where the suits hung like emptied mourners,
I looked through the shoes and the ironed handkerchiefs
And through a cardboard box full of obsolete sixpences,

I looked in the bathroom and opened the mirror,
Behind it was aspirin and dental fixative,
I looked through the drinks cabinet full of spirits,

And I found on the top of the chest-of-drawers
Where there was a photograph of my dead mother,
My living self and my accident-killed brother,

A neat plump wallet and a corroded bracelet watch
And a plate with one tooth which was hardly dry,
And I looked down the toilet and I turned

All the lights on and I turned them off,
But nowhere in the bedroom where he sat down
And fell sideways in a mysterious manner

Could I find how he did it, the conjurer
Had disappeared the trapdoor.

IV

It was easy to disappear me.
He was doing it all the time.
I did not return that bristly kiss.

On my fourth Christmas there were so many toys
I disappeared into them thoroughly,
There was a silver crane on my mother's counterpane

It was faulty but I did not want it returned,
I have reappeared and so has it,
Nearby and grown-up in the Falmouth Docks,

And there was a conjurer's set
With ping-pong balls that shucked their shells
From red to amber, amber to green,

With a black-white wand that would float,
And half-cards and split rings as tawdry
As going up on the stage among the trapdoors

And meeting Maskelyne close-up, his cuffs were soiled –
White tie and tails should be spanking clean,
My father's would have been, and I hoped

The conjurer would not kiss me,
It would disappear me.

V

He could wave his wand casually
And I would reappear elsewhere;
Once in bed at ten cuddly with mother

He waved a wand in his voice
And I got out of the silken double-cabinet
For ever.

VI

The rough kisses come round the door.
I give rough kisses myself, I am as bristly.
I am not a woman or a little boy.

And I can frighten her or make her disappear
Temporarily so she has to go to find herself
Again in the mirror somewhere;

But having learned this I am careful not to do it.
I do it less than I did.
I did not ask for this bearded equipage.

VII

It has taken me a long while
To appreciate this wedding-tackle at its worth.
My father gave it to me like a conjuring-set.

I do not use my wand to disappear you,
I am rather too fond of disappearing it myself,
But I also use it to empower us both,

It is the key to a wonderment openness
Like turning inside-out harmlessly
Among lights, turning

Over in bed into someone else.

VIII

The conjurer in his soup-and-fish
Vanishes into his cabinets,
His rival reappears, they cannot bear

To be together on the stage
Not while they're dressed in their power
Of black whiteness with starched bows

And cuffs that make the hands flash
While explaining here's a new trick:
The Chinese Cabinet.

It is a silk tent with a front door
As black and tall as Downing Street.
This must be a special trick, shall I expect

Mr Major to ride out on a white horse?
Three people with slant eyeliner have erected it,
They are dressed as spirits who seem

Of the one sex which is both sexes,
And this cabinet is not coffin-like,
No, not at all, what coffin

Would be painted with sun, moon and stars?
A Grand Mandarin with a little drum comes in,
And throws an explosive down as conjurers will

So that the tent shivers and collapses –
Yes, it is a wardrobe that has disappeared all the clothes,
The white tie and tails, the sponge-bag trousers, the soup-and-fish,

For someone is coming through stark naked
And it feels good to him
For he is laughing and the mandarin bows as if proud of him,

He who touches everywhere for all clothes are gone,
Why, he's in the buff and happy as Jesus save that
His lean rod is floating out just as it should,

Floating like my own, pleased to be like him.

FISH

Ate mackerel last night;
Dreamed of fish.

Two great fish, taller than men,
Hitched to a fishmonger's ceiling,

The tails still full and stout
Like mermaids' tails,

The scaled carcasses entirely hitched
On two Spanish queries through the upper lips,

The technicolour entrails excavated
Out of the snowy caves of flesh,

But the eyes calm and dark
As though brooding on seas far away and depths unplumbed.

As the fishmonger spoke in overalls as white
As fishflesh of fish far bigger than these,

A rich man entered and bought them both,
Had his chauffeur heave them to the car;

One was silver as ocean, the other
Golden as the rich man's abundant hair.

STAINES WATERWORKS

I

So it leaps from your taps like a fish
In its sixth and last purification
It is given a coiling motion
By the final rainbow-painted engines, which thunder;
The water is pumped free through these steel shells
Which are conched like the sea –
This is its release from the long train of events
Called *The Waterworks at Staines*.

II

Riverwater gross as gravy is filtered from
Its coarse detritus at the intake and piped
To the sedimentation plant like an Egyptian nightmare,
For it is a hall of twenty pyramids upside-down
Balanced on their points each holding two hundred and fifty
Thousand gallons making thus the alchemical sign
For water and the female triangle.

III

This reverberates like all the halls
With its engines like some moon rolling
And thundering underneath its floors, for in
This windowless hall of tides we do not see the moon.
Here the last solids fall into that sharp tip
For these twenty pyramids are decanters
And there are strong lights at their points
And when sufficient shadow has gathered the automata
Buttle their muddy jets like a river-milk
Out of the many teats of the water-sign.

In the fourth stage this more spiritual water
Is forced through anthracite beds and treated with poison gas,
The verdant chlorine which does not kill it.

V

The habitation of water is a castle, it has turrets
And doors high enough for a mounted knight in armour
To rein in, flourishing his banner, sweating his water,
To gallop along this production line of process where
There are dials to be read as though the castle library-
Books were open on reading-stands at many pages –
But these are automata and the almost-empty halls echo
Emptiness as though you walked the water-conch;
There are very few people in attendance,
All are men and seem very austere
And resemble walking crests of water in their white coats,
Hair white and long in honourable service.

VI

Their cool halls are painted blue and green
Which is the colour of the river in former times,
Purer times, in its flowing rooms.

VII

The final test is a tank of rainbow trout,
The whole station depends on it;
If the fish live, the water is good water.

VIII

In its sixth and last purification
It is given a coiling motion
By vivid yellow and conch-shaped red engines,
This gallery like the broad inside of rainbows
Which rejoice in low thunder over the purification of water,

Trumpeting Staines water triumphantly from spinning conches
    to all taps.

ESHER

The two suns,
The sun in the sea, the sun in the sky:
The bicycle of summer.

Do I deserve it,
Shirt open to my breastbone as I ride?

My shirt billowing like more lungs,
Like sunny clouds
On my summer bicycle,

The dawn wind
Smelling like a scrubbed deck.

Later, the sky of an uncolour –
Pale as a grey cat's fur,
Or ancient glassware
Rubbed misty in the desert.
Do I deserve it?

The garden birds flow up out of the lilac,
The gulls
Hang up by one wing and wheel around.

The bicyclist with all Esher
In his shirt, kept
Warm and sunny there.

LEATHER GOODS

I feel emptied by the thunderstorm. She
Looks as I feel. He takes me behind the shop
To show me the source of the leather with which
He makes his wonderful supple skirts, waistcoats,
Tabards, luggage, including doctors' bags. I must
Conceal the origin, he says, handing me her skin
Perfectly tanned, hanging it over my arm, it is heavy
As the ulster of a big man, the hands bear nails
Which are as fresh as any person's living,
I cannot see the expression, her hair
Brushes the planking. He tells me

It was a pleasure-steamer wrecked
Off the Manacles and the bones
Gently rolled out of them and their leather
Brine-tanned in a volcanic undersea stream
That was sulphurous;

'The diver into that wardrobe,
She came in one evening, when I was closing,
With a beautifully supple Gladstone bag, out of it pulled
A total body-suit with nails complete and a zip
"I can deliver five hundred," she said;
"The leather breathes, but is warm still
In sub-arctic chills," "There's
Little call for this degree
Of warm clothing here," I said,

'"Then shut your eyes," she said. I felt
A little soft cool hand steal
Into my own, it was comforting. "Let me take
Just the hands, six dozen at first, see how they go . . ."

'Under the sea the teeth rolled
Away like pearls as the gums rotted, scoured
Into white sand. The hair
Continued growing all those years, hiding the wreck
Like a head of hair itself, with full tidal tresses;
Out of that undulant harvest the diver plucked her fortune.'

BOY'S PORRIDGE

I

She serves me my round plate of porridge
Pocked with craters. It is the Full Moon
I am eating, smiling up at Mum. 'Where
Does porridge come from?' 'Down the chimney, son.'

'Why *morning* porridge?' 'It is the Moon.
We don't eat it at night. It is out of reach.'
The Moon like Santa Claus
Delivering sacks of cold porridge down the chimney.

II

My next-day's breakfast plate riding high,
Brightening the clouds. Mother pins
Her moonstone to her collar to serve me
My boy's porridge; like a full moon rising
Through maternal skies, it rides her breath.

There is cinder-snapping as the hearth-fire cools;
I go out into the night to watch the scudding
Ashes in the sky, and the round clinker riding
That burns with a cold fire. As I return

Hungry for porridge the sun rises over the sea;
Fleets of jellyfish bump in the tide
Like salty bubbles in moon-porridge
Set to boil on the hob.

TRAVELLING LIBRARY

The Iceberg Street
That leads across the Atlantic,
A west wind on the Iceberg Way:
Those books were marble,
Chilled you as you tried
To turn the pages.

Those books were smoke –
They opened and blew away
Leaving a certain tang in the air.

This is an ideal book, warm
From the last reader,
Smelling of new-baked bread
As I split its crust;

Is very nourishing
And contains as well
A certain sleep,
A certain reader's resin
Which is the rhythm of the tale
That arises to the nose
As the pages warm,

And is its bonding,
Like a cat on the lap
Sends into your belly a fire;
Now, is your friend
Whether you like it or not;
The fey body of the book,
The brightness of its tiger-heart
Which is neither
Paper or ink.

ENÝPNION

A bee in the library
Of elm books and oak books,
Holly shelves,
Ivy shelves,
The drowsy-house,
The dreamlike slumber in books;

Polishing the windows
Of the drowsy-house
That open to and fro
One sees out of the leaves;

I open the book and its honey runs over,
The supple binding polished with beeswax,
The dark-veined pages,
The whispering leaves
Inscribed with sentences that hum
In the amber twilight,

A gentleman's library
In which to drowse
That is full of Virgil
Who has retired,
Who has finished with all
Heroes larger than beesize.

NUDE STUDIES VI: THE HORSE

She is in love with the canoe-faces of horses,
Their violin smile. Riding them
Naked skin to skin

Is to sail close to the symphonic brink of the known world.
It amazes her that entering the pub
Of kisses, basket meals, stout decals, accelerando

Chatter, is to plunge
Into a rubbish-tip of bright plastic and broken
Radio-sets still working though they

Have been thrown away; yet after a beer or two
It is eating one's Good Food inside a Christmas Tree;
And this marvel is nothing

To the sonorous breathing of the horse
She rode yesterday skin to skin
Up to the vast water-note

Of the reservoir from which the horse
As from a harp plucked water; the ripples
Of his drink reached out easily to the far shore.

SALE

The fever had passed.
She felt cool and dry.
She asked: 'Why
Don't we take a drive
Over the hills?' It was perhaps
Too soon after the fire.
Mother was ironing palls,
And the lake was shaking the hills.

There had been a cellar-fire
Breaking through the racks
Of dust-and-spiderweb-silted
Bottles,

Caused by the old liqueurs
Starting to work again,
For the flame was wildfire
Like brandy-flame
Blue as electricity
That does not scorch the hand;

The fire was harmless and amazing,
Like the round flame of a Christmas pudding,
Clasping the church roof,
Flapping over it like a pall.

The sparks from a shattered bottle
Igniting the webs – spider-fire?

Were the firemen still hosing?
There was nothing to hose, no.
They have disappeared into the rectory
Leaving behind that aura
Which hangs around shut-down machinery.

Mother said: 'Your sons
Could help on the farm,
Your daughters in the house,
Filling the place
With friendly faces.'

Daddy lifted her up
And swung her round again.
The bright lake
Blinded her when he did that,
The lake that carried over its surface
Like a loudspeaker made of water
The dislocated sounds of trucks
Rumbling out over the overpass.

It was a dissonance
Which changed the look of the water
That magnified it. A winter look
Now of cold fragments where peak
Would not connect with lake,
Lake would not reflect peak
And shivered it,
Gave it the water's trembling
That solid rock
Blurred by the matt waves. As these lorries
Passed through the town the shopwindows
Cursed at them in French: SALE SALE SALE.

ABATTOIR BRIDE

Slow-working in the slaughterhouse
On a showery day. He holds out
A bloody fillet in his icy hands.
I pop with sweat. Bleed out, sparkle!

There are flies like lacquered idols, skulls
The size of sand-grains humming like nuns,
Exquisite religious sculpture vibrating
To the note of that god-gong, the sun,
Flies carved again as with knives, risen
Out of the food-chest with ivory clasps,
Shut into the meat, it seems, by him let out
With his shining knives and his shadow of flies,
His marriage-property, sturdy and obscene.

And there is a leaf-marriage too, the sun lying
In panels and yellow shadows on the path,
The flies in intermediary shady swarms
Celebrating the marriage of meat and sun;

And this little rain marries all the leaves;
The sealed chamber, this vagina
Is like a bird flying
Through the rain, drenched,
Beak wide as a fledgling straining for the worm;

He has opened many creatures, this one
Opens itself, alive, without violation,
However loud the sun, with its darkening flies.